# bathroom stuff

holman **wang**

**photography by**
**t.j. adel & son**

**SOURCEBOOKS, INC.**
NAPERVILLE, ILLINOIS

Published by Sourcebooks, Inc.
P.O. Box 4410, Naperville, Illinois  60567-4410
(630) 961-3900
FAX: (630) 961-2168
ISBN 1-57071-651-X (duck)
ISBN 1-57071-790-7 (soaps)
ISBN 1-57071-789-3 (toothbrush)
ISBN 1-57071-791-5 (faucet)

Library of Congress Cataloging-in-Publication Data
Wang, Holman.
    Bathroom stuff / by Holman Wang.
        p. cm.
        (alk. paper)
1. Bathrooms—Equipment and supplies—History. 2. Toilet preparations—History. 3. Cosmetics—History. 4. Drugs—History. I. Title.

TX303.W35 2001
668'.22—dc21
00-066171

Printed and bound in the United States of America
DO   10   9   8   7   6   5   4   3   2   1

# dedication

For those who had faith in me

# acknowledgments

## Special thanks to:

• Ted and Sam at T. J. Adel & Son for their fantastic photography and good humor • Robert at Contemporary Management for keeping my proposal out of the slush pile • Todd and the staff at Sourcebooks for their enthusiasm and energy • Jack for editing the chapters in the early stages • Jason for suggesting the "fun facts" format • Kerry for lending me her bathroom stuff • Joe for pointing out the cultural importance of Brylcreem • My parents and my grandmother for their support and encouragement •

## Thanks to:

• The friendly and helpful staff at the Vancouver Public Library Central Branch • Jason at Robinson Lighting • Lisa at Absolutely Diapers • Steve and Laura at Bullnose Tile and Stone • Tricia at Everbrite Denture Clinic • Linda and Paul at Ashley House Wallcoverings Inc. • Steve at Motiv Design • Carly and Caroline at Greetings Etc. • Kevin at Home Depot • Sarah at Rieva and Reine The Lifestyle Store • Carol Sandler at the Strong Museum (Manhattan) •

# permissions

# table of contents

# introduction

The bathroom's rise to prominence in the modern home is nothing short of miraculous. In the early 1800s, the bathroom as we know it simply did not exist. Not even Buckingham Palace or the White House had one. People bathed in various rooms in large buckets, assuming they bathed at all. If a family was lucky enough to have a tub, it usually did double duty as a laundry basin. And going to the toilet was an outdoor affair, except on cold days when a chamber pot was used for convenience.

From these unpromising origins, the bathroom has transformed over the last two centuries into a lavish mecca of personal well-being. Today, the bathroom not only has a sink, bath, and toilet, but also a full arsenal of gadgets and elixirs designed to primp our bodies and pamper our souls. For those of us who yearn for creature comforts, life without the bathroom is unimaginable.

Every one of us has an intimate relationship with our bathroom; it's where we perform many of our most personal rituals. Yet, the stuff that fills our bathrooms has become such an ordinary part of our lives that we take it for granted. So it's time to rediscover and celebrate all the little things that have changed our world for the better, from the unassuming toothbrush to the humble roll of toilet paper.

A look at the history of these everyday objects also uncovers a fascinating history of humankind. The story of the bathroom reveals our eccentricities, our foibles, and most importantly, our uncanny knack for inventive genius. After all, it's centuries of toil and innovation that has transformed the bathroom from a lowly architectural afterthought into a modern shrine to health and happiness—and the most indispensable room in the home today.

# acne remedies

Through the ages, treating acne largely has been a quack endeavor. Tutankhamen, the teenaged Pharaoh with a pimple problem, likely used a popular Egyptian remedy made of milk, olive oil, sea salt, ostrich eggs, and bull's bile—but to no avail. The Romans used a paste of barley flour and butter with equally dismal results. Though ancient texts contained countless recipes for complexion creams, the use of sulfur is the only treatment that has survived to the present from classical times.

In the 1700s, British surgeon Daniel Turner wrote that treating acne was not below the dignity of a doctor. While his heart was in the right place, his science was not—Turner blamed acne on hard drinking. Besides getting off the bottle, he also prescribed bleeding by lancet or leeches and topical creams containing lead or mercury. Antacids and laxatives were also fashionable remedies since acne often was viewed as a symptom of digestive disorder. Strangely, some of Turner's contemporaries believed that bad skin was actually a sign of good health, reasoning that pimples were caused by poisons leaving the body.

Acne treatments remained crude through to the early 1900s. Sulfur was still an old standby, but dermatologists often prescribed suspect cures containing dried thyroid or arsenic. Another common treatment was a twelve-week course of X-ray exposures to the face.

Things only began changing for the better in 1939 when Canadian doctor William Pace began studying benzoyl peroxide, a mainstay of acne therapy up to today. In 1949, American Ivan DeBlois Combe created Clearasil, which became a household name after the skin-toned cream was advertised on the teenage dance show *American Bandstand* in 1957. Nowadays, a host of effective acne-fighters are at our disposal, including retinoids and antibiotics. And here's more good news: people should never fear eating chocolate, pizza, fries, or nuts. There is no proven link between eating certain foods and breaking out.

## late bloomer

The word "acne" first appeared in the sixth century in the writings of Aëtius Amidenus, physician to the Byzantine Emperor Justinian. The term was confined to medical dictionaries, and only came into general use in the nineteenth century.

2

**NEW**

multi-action
astringent

*Fast acting, long-lasting*

- unclogs pores
- deep cleans
- fights pimples

2% SALICYLIC ACID ACNE MEDICATION

8.0 fl oz (236ml)

## true colors

For centuries, people believed that blackheads were darkened by airborne dirt. This myth was dispelled in 1956 when it was found that blackheads are actually colored by our own skin pigment, melanin.

## chewing the fat

Africans have treated blemishes for thousands of years with shea butter, a thick fat from the seeds of the West African shea tree. Since shea butter is also an important source of food, cutting down the shea tree is illegal in most of West Africa.

## wanted side effect

Scientists discovered in the 1990s that tretinoin, a vitamin A derivative used to fight acne, could reverse some of the effects of photo-aging, such as fine wrinkles, freckles, and larger blotches known as "liver spots."

## wistful thinking

Eight out of ten people will get pimples at some point in their lives. Seventy-nine percent of teenage boys and 89 percent of teenage girls list acne as one of their biggest worries, and nearly 60 percent of those age fifteen to twenty-four think about their acne at least once a day.

## french dressing

A fifteenth century French recipe for acne cream called for asparagus roots, white lily bulbs, wild anise, and goat's milk. The concoction was aged in warm horse manure and then filtered through felt.

# allergy medicines

When King Menes of Egypt died from an insect sting in the third millennium b.c., allergies and other mysterious afflictions were thought to be the handiwork of incensed gods. A real understanding of allergies didn't begin until 1819 when Englishman John Bostock made the first clinical description of "summer discharge"—what we now call hay fever. It was considered rare at the time, and one of Bostock's colleagues even suggested hay fever was "confined to the upper classes of society." Absurd as this observation seems, it may have had some merit. Today, the number of allergy sufferers in wealthy nations is ballooning, while people in India, Eastern Russia, and rural Africa—places with no shortage of airborne irritants—are far less troubled by allergies. Watery eyes and runny noses are supposed to protect our bodies by flushing out pathogens. However, the ultra-hygienic environments engendered by high living standards may have left our immune systems with so little to do they wind up overreacting to harmless substances such as latex, pollen, dust, or dander.

A crucial step towards allergy relief was taken in 1907 when researchers found that allergens trigger the release of histamine, which in turn causes wheezing and sneezing. Hoping to find a way to block histamine's action, Swiss pharmacologist Daniel Bovet conducted some three thousand experiments in the 1930s and '40s. He succeeded in 1944, creating the world's first antihistamine. A year later, scientists created diphenhydramine, the popular drug best known today as Benadryl. Unfortunately, this older type of antihistamine causes sedation, which studies show can impair driving and learning. Non-drowsy formulas solve the problem by using larger molecules that are unable to pass into the brain. Other allergy-fighters include decongestants and steroids, and more advanced treatments continue to be researched. This is good news since some experts are convinced that half of the people in the industrialized world are now allergic to something.

## big budget production

The money ($400 million) spent on just two classes of allergy medicine, steroid nasal sprays and non-drowsy antihistamines, accounted for three-quarters of the total spent on prescription drug ads in medical journals in 1999.

## bad air day

The United States is the world's largest market for allergy medication. Allergies cost the country two million days of lost schooling, three million days of lost work, six million days of bed rest, twenty-eight million days of restricted activity, and $2 billion in treatments.

## fishy circumstances

Anaphylaxis, a severe allergic reaction that can lead to shock and death, was first described by two French scientists in 1902. They accidentally discovered that minute amounts of jellyfish toxins caused lethal allergic reactions in dogs.

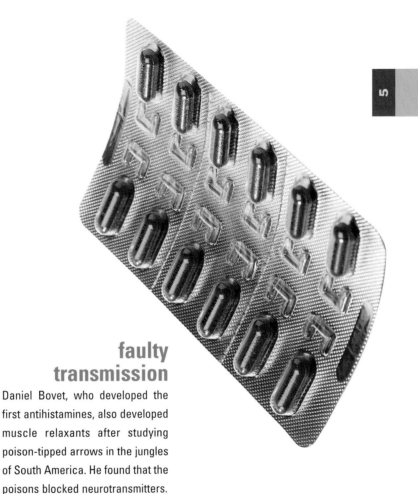

## faulty transmission

Daniel Bovet, who developed the first antihistamines, also developed muscle relaxants after studying poison-tipped arrows in the jungles of South America. He found that the poisons blocked neurotransmitters.

## culinary cures

Garlic, onions, and real licorice all contain anti-inflammatory compounds. A natural antihistamine also can be found in many fruits and vegetables: vitamin C.

## a real downer

Some over-the-counter antihistamines can cause drowsiness and impair motor skills. Studies show that even recommended doses can cause sedation that is equivalent to being legally drunk.

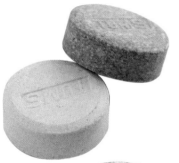

# antacids

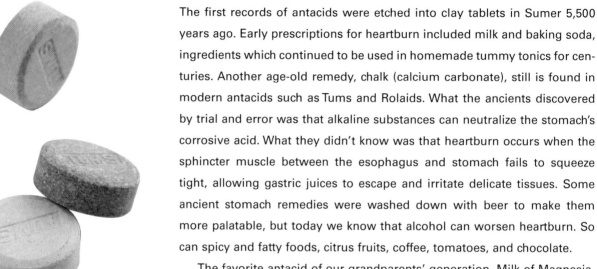

The first records of antacids were etched into clay tablets in Sumer 5,500 years ago. Early prescriptions for heartburn included milk and baking soda, ingredients which continued to be used in homemade tummy tonics for centuries. Another age-old remedy, chalk (calcium carbonate), still is found in modern antacids such as Tums and Rolaids. What the ancients discovered by trial and error was that alkaline substances can neutralize the stomach's corrosive acid. What they didn't know was that heartburn occurs when the sphincter muscle between the esophagus and stomach fails to squeeze tight, allowing gastric juices to escape and irritate delicate tissues. Some ancient stomach remedies were washed down with beer to make them more palatable, but today we know that alcohol can worsen heartburn. So can spicy and fatty foods, citrus fruits, coffee, tomatoes, and chocolate.

The favorite antacid of our grandparents' generation, Milk of Magnesia, was created by Charles Phillips in Connecticut in 1873. The antacid's recipe called for a suspension of magnesium hydroxide in water, and the resulting liquid looked like milk. Although the product was wildly popular, in larger doses it produced an undesired laxative effect. This problem was solved in 1949 with the launch of Maalox. The makers of Maalox shrewdly combined magnesium hydroxide with another common antacid, aluminum hydroxide, which induced unwanted constipation. The two chemicals effectively cancelled out each other's side effects, and many of today's antacids continue to exploit this bowel-friendly combination.

Studies show that 7 percent of people suffer heartburn daily, 14 percent weekly, and 15 percent monthly, meaning 36 percent of people have chronic heartburn. The highest rates, however, are found in pregnant women. Because estrogen can weaken sphincter muscles and babies can push their mothers' organs out of place, 25 percent of pregnant women suffer heartburn daily.

## GI blues

In the United States, gastrointestinal (GI) disorders result in two hundred thousand absences from work every day. This costs government and businesses at least $50 billion a year.

## something to chew on

For mild cases of heartburn, help may be found in chewing gum. Chewing gum increases saliva flow, which can protect the esophagus from corrosive stomach acids.

## plop plop fizz fizz

Effervescent Alka-Seltzer tablets were launched in the United States in 1931. The repeal of Prohibition in 1933 sent sales of Alka-Seltzer skyrocketing after the product gained a reputation as a sure fix for hangovers.

## flotation device

Some heartburn remedies contain alginate, which is not an antacid. It is a tasteless substance made from seaweed. When swallowed, alginate floats on top of gastric fluids and prevents acids from escaping the stomach.

## un-magnetic personality

Pepto-Bismol, launched in 1919, contains bismuth, a metallic element resistant to hydrochloric acid that was first described by a German monk in 1450. Incidentally, bismuth is the metal that exhibits the greatest opposition to being magnetized.

## mint condition

Peppermint relieves flatulence by stimulating burps, hence the custom of eating after-dinner mints. Peppermint relaxes the lower esophageal sphincter, releasing gas, but this also can allow acid to creep up the esophagus and cause heartburn.

# antibiotics

In March of 1942, Anne Miller was lying in a hospital bed in Connecticut with a raging fever. The bacterial infection that was coursing through Miller's body left her delirious and near death. Having exhausted all conventional therapies, her doctors asked for a "miracle drug" that had been developed in England but had never been used on an American patient. Only a teaspoon of it arrived in a small bottle, and interns were given one clear instruction about the drug: not to drop it on the floor. The injections began on a Saturday afternoon. By Sunday morning, Miller's temperature was suddenly back to normal, and a few hours later, she was all but her old self again. Her doctors were overjoyed, sensing that Miller's improbable escape from death would mark a critical turning point in medical history.

That turning point was the introduction of antibiotics, and the drug that saved Miller's life was penicillin. As the famous story goes, Alexander Fleming accidentally discovered penicillin in London in 1928 when a mold blew in through a window and killed bacteria in an open petri dish. Fleming dismissed the medical potential of his own findings at first, but others would pick up where his research left off.

Around the start of World War II, a team at Oxford University began testing penicillin on mice with convincing results. In early 1941, human trials began. More encouraging results proved to scientists that penicillin was ready for mass-production. However, they were so fearful of a German attack on England that they smeared the precious penicillin mold on their coat linings to preserve a secret supply, and decided to shift production of the drug to the United States. When Anne Miller fell ill, penicillin was rushed from a New Jersey lab, and Miller soon became the first resounding antibiotics success story. Though Fleming had never treated Miller, he came to visit her in the U.S. and gushed, "Thank you, Mrs. Miller. You are my most important patient."

## going flat out

Since penicillin grew best in shallow containers, the mold was cultured by early researchers in lab dishes, pie plates, serving trays, cookie tins, and bedpans.

## civil war

The antibiotic effect was first observed by Frenchmen Louis Pasteur and Jules-François Jouvert in 1877. They discovered that common-air bacteria could kill the bacteria responsible for anthrax.

## chivalrous

Alexander Fleming discovered penicillin in 1928, but modestly insisted that others were more responsible for its development as a medical treatment. Nevertheless, he garnered twenty-five honorary degrees, won the Nobel Prize, and was knighted.

## man-eater

Just before antibiotics were launched in the 1940s, the use of maggots to eat away infected flesh was becoming an effective and popular medical treatment. Fueled by concerns over antibiotics resistance, interest in maggot-therapy is growing again.

## scrimping and saving

Precious little penicillin was available when the first human trial was conducted. In order not to waste penicillin, the patient's urine was collected so that the drug could be recovered in a lab and reused.

## unwitting antibiotics

To treat infections, the early Chinese used moldy soybean curds, the Mayans used cuxum fungi, while the Egyptians used yeast from sweet beer. A seventeenth century English recipe for an anti-infection unguent even called for "moss from dead men's skulls."

# antiperspirant

## claim to fame

Human beings are the most intelligent creatures in the animal kingdom—and the sweatiest. In a hot desert, a person can lose over two gallons of sweat in a day.

In Elizabethan England, lovers partook in a curious custom: they exchanged peeled apples that had been worn under their armpits. Back then, sweat was considered something of an aphrodisiac, but underarm wetness has since been banished—along with all other forms of bodily excreta—into the realm of the socially embarrassing. Sweat is actually quite wholesome—it's 99 percent water with traces of salts and amino acids—but for many of us nothing could be more disgraceful than being caught with two soggy circles blotting our best shirt.

The first true antiperspirant, Everdry, was put on the market in the United States in 1902 and peddled exclusively to women—ironic since men are the more prolific sweat producers. Everdry contained a solution of aluminum chloride salts, which stung the skin. Antiperspirant formulas remained harsh until the early 1950s when Arrid used buffered salts to create a significantly milder sweat-fighter. It didn't irritate the skin, and just as importantly, it didn't eat through clothes. Arrid antiperspirant soon became a bestseller for both women and men, but even satisfied customers didn't exactly rave to their friends about the breakthrough technology. At the time, underarm sweat was still a touchy topic of conversation. When the first roll-on antiperspirant, Mum Rollette, debuted in 1952, the British were so prudish about wetness protection that their TV ad for Mum—unlike the American version—showed the product rolled on the arm rather than the underarm.

Researchers have worked on antiperspirants for more than a century, but even industry insiders admit that no one knows exactly how they work. It is thought that aluminum salts either plug up sweat glands like corks or cause the skin around the glands to puff up, thereby preventing perspiration from leaking. But as long as sweat is tamed and disgrace is averted, people probably couldn't care less about the science behind it.

SHAKE WELL BEFORE USING

### the main attraction

Scientific studies suggest that sweat and the odor associated with it may be responsible for attracting mosquitoes, blackflies, and other bite-happy insects. The studies further suggest that sweat from the groin is a particularly potent attractant.

### breaking the smell barrier

Early antiperspirants were given euphemistic names such as Everdry, Mum, and Hush. The first antiperspirant to exuberantly announce its purpose was Odo-Ro-No, which debuted in 1914. Five years later, it was the first brand to mention "B.O." in its ads.

### he shed, she shed

Men and women sweat differently. Women mainly sweat from under their arms, but men also sweat from the back, chest, and temples. A woman's sweat can also be up to fourteen times more alkaline than a man's.

### slowly but surely

The 1930s saw the introduction of slow-drying antiperspirants. The sweat-fighting solutions tested people's patience by taking fifteen minutes to "set," but offered wetness protection for three or four days.

### hot and unbothered

U.S. Air Force experiments have revealed that sweating allows naked humans to endure air temperatures up to an astounding 400° F. It only takes 325° F to cook meat.

# aspirin

Long before doctors told patients to take two aspirin and call in the morning, our ancient ancestors were using natural versions of the drug to fight pain and fever. Plants containing salicin, a variant of aspirin, were known to the early Egyptians, Greeks, Chinese, and native North Americans. Painkilling potions were usually brewed from willow bark, and Hippocrates even prescribed them to relieve the agony of childbirth. However, harsh side effects such as nausea and stomach ulcers were common.

The road to a safer painkiller was first paved by German scientists who isolated salicin from willow bark in 1828. By the mid-1800s, several European chemists had synthesized a far less noxious form, acetylsalicylic acid, or ASA. However, their work was never commercially exploited and soon faded into obscurity. The glory of "discovering" ASA—later named Aspirin—was instead reaped by German chemist Felix Hoffman.

Hoffman was working for Bayer in 1897 when he began searching for a gentler pain reliever to ease his father's rheumatism. The elder Hoffman was taking a salicin derivative that had eaten away at his stomach, and he begged his son to find a better cure. Drawing on earlier research, Hoffman was soon able to synthesize ASA, and it cured his father's pain without serious side effects. Instead of being swiftly hailed as a new wonder drug, however, ASA languished on Bayer's shelves for more than a year. At the time, Bayer was busy promoting its other wonder drug: heroin. Marketed as safe and non-addictive, heroin was used to soothe everything from coughs to crying babies. Bayer returned its attention to ASA only after doctors who had been secretly given free samples of the drug began writing glowing reports. In 1899, ASA was finally presented to the world under the brand name Aspirin. It quickly became the world's most prescribed drug and remains popular today—the average person in a developed country pops one hundred aspirins every year.

## name game

Some suggest the name aspirin derives from *Spiraea*, the genus of plants from which acetylsalicylic acid is made. Others contend that aspirin is named in honor of St. Aspirinius, the patron saint of headaches.

12

## rubbing it in

Pliny, the Roman historian, suggested rubbing crushed snails on the forehead as a cure for headache. Mexicans in the Sierra Madres did the same with live toads, while sixth century French bishop St. Gregory rubbed his head against St. Martin's tomb.

## for art's sake

Curious ailments documented by medical journals include Academy Headache, described by British doctors in the late nineteenth century as severe head pain, sleeplessness, and anxiety caused by studying picture collections in art galleries.

## bad blood

Milder forms of vascular headaches—head pains caused by swollen blood vessels—can be triggered by extremely high blood pressure, fever, hunger, and even sexual orgasm.

## to the victor go the spoils

The brand name Aspirin was a trademark of the Bayer company until Germany's defeat in World War I. The trademark was handed over to the Allies in 1919 as war reparations at the Treaty of Versailles.

## metamorphosis

Czech novelist Franz Kafka, tortured by existential angst, told his fiancée that aspirin was one of the few things that could transform his painful state of being into a happier one.

# bandages

In prehistoric times, our cave dwelling cousins covered their wounds with simple dressings of mud, leaves, or animal hide. Later on, cotton and other fabrics became the materials of choice. Early writings show that cloth bandages were used in China, Mesopotamia, Egypt, Greece, and Rome. Hippocrates, for example, prescribed a clean linen cloth soaked in wine or vinegar for covering wounds. However, many Greek doctors argued instead that wounds should be allowed to form pus as part of the healing process. As late as the 1300s, followers of the "laudable pus" tradition spurned bandaging in favor of opening and reopening wounds until pus oozed out. Another grisly treatment was cauterization, done by pouring boiling oil or placing red hot blades into wounds. This stopped bleeding by burning and coagulating flesh. Not surprisingly, many patients preferred crackpot "magical" cures over visits to the surgeon. Cautery was finally abandoned when French physician Ambroise Paré reintroduced the idea of bandaging wounds in the sixteenth century.

The art of wound healing was revolutionized in the twentieth century by the invention of adhesive bandages. They were first introduced by Johnson & Johnson in 1921 as Band-Aids—a name now recognized the world over. Earle Dickson, a company employee, dreamt up the product for his danger-prone wife. Tired of constantly dressing her cuts and burns from cooking, Dickson decided to make a bandage that his wife could put on herself. He laid out a long strip of surgical tape sticky-side up on a table and placed small squares of gauze on it at intervals. Dickson then used crinoline to cover the sticky portions. Whenever his wife needed to dress a wound, she simply removed the crinoline, cut off a piece of tape, and applied it as a bandage. When Dickson showed his idea to his bosses, they loved it. Eighty years and one hundred billion Band-Aids later, clearly, so do we.

## band width

The first Band-Aids, made by hand, were 2½ inches wide and an unwieldy 18 inches long. The now familiar ¾ inch by 3 inch size was first introduced when production was mechanized in 1924.

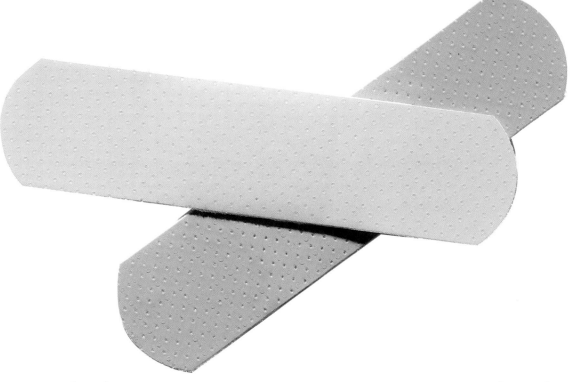

### hard core wrap

The Egyptians not only used bandages to dress wounds, but also to embalm the dead. Higher ranking individuals received finer wrappings, and up to three hundred yards of linen bandages were used to wrap one mummy.

### on the fly

A Second World War American bombing crew that landed safely after an in-flight emergency owed their lives to Band-Aids. The crew used the adhesive bandages to repair leaks in the damaged hydraulic system.

### chop shop

To promote Band-Aids when the product was first launched, Johnson & Johnson gave out free samples to Boy Scouts across the U.S. One enterprising salesman from Cleveland even handed out free Band-Aids to every butcher in town.

### off again, on again

In the days before bacteriology, physicians did not know to protect their patients from infection. Disastrously, bandages and dressings often were reused again and again.

### web technology

At the Battle of Crecy in 1346, English archers stopped their wounds from bleeding by laying spider webs over them.

# bath oils

In the hectic modern world, we could all use a little more pampering. Since most of us can't jet off to a resort spa at the first sign of stress, taking a long hot bath is the next best thing. Nearly one in three women see a bath as a way to "indulge," not just get clean. And to create a sense of escape in their own home, more and more women are locking their bathroom doors, turning down the lights, and scenting bath water with essential oils.

Perfumed baths are an age-old pleasure. In ancient Egypt, baths were scented with hyacinth and honeysuckle, while in India, brides-to-be from prominent families spent long hours in fragrant baths every day for a month before their weddings. Hippocrates even prescribed perfumed baths for good health. The ancients believed that smells were not only pleasant, but therapeutic. This belief, however, waned in the late nineteenth century. At the Paris International Exhibition in 1867, perfumes and soaps were exhibited apart from the pharmacy section for the first time, thus divorcing "cosmetics" from their medicinal roots. But in the early 1900s, French chemist Henri Gattefosse rediscovered the heath benefits of fragrant oils after burning his hand in his lab. He thrust his hand into the nearest cool liquid, a vat of lavender oil, and was so impressed with how quickly his burn healed that he devoted the rest of his life to the study of essential oils. Gattefosse was fascinated by the healing powers of smell, and coined the term "aromatherapy" in 1928.

## all that jas

Forty-five minutes of picking yields five thousand jasmine flowers, which weigh about a pound. Extracting one pound of jasmine oil, however, takes about eight hundred pounds of flowers.

Aromatherapy advocates claim a strong whiff of a good scent can do everything from calm nerves to boost libido (in fact, more and more companies are making unisex bath oils for amorous couples). Critics of aromatherapy abound, but studies show smell does change mood faster than any other form of sensory perception. The effects may be psychological rather than physiological, but most people probably don't care to quibble about the science. They just want a long, hot soak in the tub to wash their worries away.

### love's labors launched

Bathing salts have been collected from the Dead Sea for centuries. King Solomon gave salts to his lover, the Queen of Sheba, while Cleopatra persuaded Mark Antony to launch a conquest of the region to guarantee her a steady source of bathing supplies.

### going to the dogs

When conventional remedies fail to rid dogs of their fleas, some pet owners and vets spray their dogs with diluted Avon bath oils. Anecdotal evidence suggests this helps keep Fido flea-free.

### take a bite out of grime

Soap scum, skin cells, dirt, and bath oils can form a residue in whirlpool pipes that can eventually shoot out as black goo. To avoid this, whirlpools should be "purged" every three months with hot water and crystal dishwashing detergent.

### baby your baby

Some upscale cosmetics producers have introduced aromatherapy bath oils for babies featuring chamomile and lavender to calm fussy newborns. Parents, however, should be careful. Babies can be allergic to any product—even natural ones.

### fit for a king

Some high-end bath oils contain frankincense, an aromatic gum resin. In biblical times, frankincense was costlier than gold, and likely the most precious substance on earth.

Olio da Bagno
Bath Oil

Sandalo
Sandalwood

# bath toys

Toys have charmed kids since the dawn of civilization, and luring children into washing with the promise of bath time fun is no doubt a time-honored bit of parental trickery. The earliest bathing enticements were likely boats. Those made by seafaring peoples were not only playthings, but also teaching tools used to pass on vital shipbuilding skills to children. For example, toy canoes made by native peoples near the Great Lakes displayed all the key construction details—lashings, ribs, and bark strips—of full-sized canoes.

Most ancient cultures had toys, but toy-making as an industry did not emerge until the sixteenth century when the first major toy centers arose in Germany. Early boats were made of wood, but as German forests declined during the industrial revolution, toy-makers turned to cast-iron and tin-plate—materials perfect for model warships. Boats made of celluloid, an early type of plastic, debuted in the 1890s. Germany was the biggest producer of plastic toys before World War I, but by war's end, this title was seized by Japan.

The precise origin of that other ubiquitous bath toy, the yellow rubber duck, has been lost to the mists of time. We do know, however, that rubber toys enjoyed great popularity after 1839 when Charles Goodyear began making a more elastic and durable form of rubber. The New York Rubber Company was one of the first toy-makers to exploit this new material. By the mid-1800s, their most sought-after product may have been rubber squeak toys that blew air out of a whistle when squeezed, and the rubber duck was likely unveiled around this time. The yellow bath buddy became firmly ensconced in bathroom culture when Ernie and the "Rubber Duckie" song debuted on Sesame Street in 1970.

So what do children like better in the bathtub, boats or rubber ducks? According to an American survey, 26 percent of kids under six prefer boats, edging out the 22 percent who are "awfully fond" of their rubber duckies.

## jumping ship

In 1992, a container fell off a ship in the middle of the Pacific, releasing twenty-nine thousand rubber ducks and other bath toys. The toys began washing up on shore in North America eleven months later, and their journey helped scientists study ocean currents.

## bread and water

Since water symbolized purity, it was not uncommon in Medieval Europe for wedding ceremonies to take place in a bath. Up to a dozen people would stand half-submerged in a large tub, and food was served on toy boats.

## weekend warriors

Noah's Arks made of wood were popular toys centuries ago—in and out of the water. Many have survived in good condition, and some say this is because children only played with the arks on Sundays.

## fair is fowl and fowl is fair

Celebriducks, a Silicon Valley-based maker of bath toys, sells rubber ducks sporting celebrity faces, including Groucho Marx, Babe Ruth, the Mona Lisa, and Shakespeare.

## sesame street crash

When the "Rubber Duckie" song was performed by the Boston Pops, the orchestra members were not permitted to squeeze rubber ducks without extra pay since the ducks were considered second instruments. In the end, only the percussion section squeaked the ducks.

## sesame street smash

In 1996, a German Ernie singing in German made the "Rubber Duckie" song a smash hit in—you guessed it—Germany. A CD with five different versions of the tune, including a dance remix, sold nearly two million copies.

# bathroom scales

Most of us expend three to four hundred fewer calories of energy a day than people did fifty years ago. Our sedentary modern lifestyles, along with richer diets, have lead to paunchier guts, flabbier thighs, and a love-hate relationship between people and their bathroom scales.

Scales were invented in the Middle East as early as 4000 b.c. The simplest were equal-arm scales with two pans hanging from either end of a pivoting beam (the zodiac sign for Libra). These scales, however, were used to weigh goods, not people. The first step towards the bathroom scale was not taken until Leonardo da Vinci invented the first self-indicating scale around 1500. When goods were placed in a pan, a semi-circular chart acting as a pendulum would swing. Weight was then read off markings on the chart against a fixed pointer—the way we still read many bathroom scales today. In the eighteenth and nineteenth centuries, the growth of toll roads, railway shipping, and postal services (which all charged by weight) helped spur advances in scale technology. Spring scales were invented in this period. Many of today's bathroom scales employ spring mechanisms which, depending on the degree they are stretched or compressed, turn a circular dial that gives us our weight.

## power failure

Gravity affects weight, but it is an extremely weak force. If gravity had the same power as the force that pulls oppositely charged matter together, your bathroom scale would display your weight in a forty-digit number.

Bathroom scales became popular in the early 1900s as people became increasingly weight-conscious. In 1907, health experts introduced the now-ubiquitous idea of calorie-counting. Insurance companies coined the term "ideal weight" in 1923 and began charging portly policyholders higher premiums. The first "lite" beer was launched in 1975, and the 1980s saw a flood of low-cal and low-fat foods hit supermarket shelves. Today, with thin bodies glamorized in the media, weight-consciousness has turned into obsession—50 percent of women and 25 percent of men in the U.S. are on diets. Contrary to popular belief, however, Americans are not the heaviest people on earth. Western Samoans are, but Americans do lead the industrialized world.

## sacred cows

Many early weights used for beam balances took on animal forms. The ancient Egyptians, who often used scales in religious rituals, favored weights shaped like cows.

## for hearts' sake

Sudden weight gains can be dangerous for people with heart trouble. To monitor the situation, some patients weigh themselves daily on special home scales that can relay results to doctors via wireless technology.

## no ulterior motives

If you think carnal pleasures can help you lose weight, think again. The average adult expends about seventeen thousand calories a year during sex, which sheds less than five pounds.

## through thick and thin

High-tech bathroom scales can measure body fat by sending an imperceptible electrical signal through your body. Since the signal passes faster through muscle and slower through fat, measuring its speed against one's height and weight reveals fat levels.

## weighty issues

The sixteen-ounce pound was first popularized in Norman England (1066–1154). Metric weight standards were developed in France during the Revolution (1789–1799) since each province had its own weight measures—a chaotic situation revolutionaries blamed on "feudal maladministration."

# baths

The first purpose-built bathtub was made around 1800 B.C. for King Minos in the Cretan Palace of Knossos. The clay tub was large enough to recline in, but had no drain and needed to be filled and bailed by hand. The Greeks did build tubs with drains, but people crouched rather than lounged in the shallow fixtures. In Rome, private bathing was rare. People frequented the elaborate system of public baths, with the most indulgent bathers making several trips a day. While Roman bodies were clean, their minds were not. Public baths earned a reputation for debauchery, which enraged the budding Christian Church.

After Rome was sacked in the fifth century a.d., bathing in Europe fell into disrepute. Christian leaders taught that exposing the flesh to bathe was sinful. Ironically, the act of bathing was enjoyed by monks and nuns who felt that nudity would not lead them astray as it would laymen. Bathing did enjoy a brief vogue in medieval times, but fell out of favor again after public baths were blamed for spreading plague and disease. The Reformation of the 1500s dealt bathing another blow as Catholics and Protestants started a piety contest, with each group trying to outdo the other by revealing as little flesh as possible to bathwater. By the colonial era, Europeans were often far dirtier than the "savages" they subjugated.

Attitudes towards bathing and hygiene changed after cholera decimated European cities in the early 1800s. The British began making claw-foot tubs out of porcelain by mid-century, followed by cheaper cast-iron tubs. In 1911, the Kohler Company launched a bathtub set flat on the floor, since cleaning underneath claw-foot tubs was difficult. This design encouraged the standardized five-foot wall recess we still see today. People bathed once a week or less before 1950 (families often took turns using the same bathwater), but after World War II, bathing became an Occidental obsession. Americans and Canadians now lead the way, claiming to bathe or shower more than seven times a week.

## how the other half lived

While Europeans stank during the Middle Ages, others kept the torch of hygiene burning. The Moors built sumptuous public baths called *hammam*, and Marco Polo commented on the cleanliness of the Chinese, who also enjoyed the use of public baths.

### double take

Bathing was so important to the ancient Cretans that they were often buried in terra-cotta coffins that were indistinguishable from bathtubs, except for the addition of a lid. Some even had drain holes.

### c.o.d.

Wealthy nineteenth century Parisians, particularly women who didn't dare undress in public baths, could have baths delivered to their door. Horse-drawn wagons arrived with barrels of hot water, portable tubs, and bathrobes.

### on the hot seat

The ancient Aztecs cleaned themselves in steam baths, while some Native American tribes used sweat lodges. During the Dark Ages, saunas developed in Finland and Russia, countries where the anti-bathing Christian Church was slow to establish itself.

### soaked

Religious dictates and the abundance of natural hot springs have made bathing an important tradition in Japan. Some people even bathe in sake (rice wine), a practice that dates back three thousand years.

### getting the boot

In 1790, Benjamin Franklin brought the first bathtub to the United States from Europe after a stint as ambassador to France. The "slipper bath" looked like a giant boot, with a firebox to heat water under the heel and a drain at the toe.

# bidets

If someone asks why there's a children's drinking fountain beside the toilet, that person is probably an American who has never before set eyes—let alone their rear end—on a bidet. Americans who dare use one often find it a danger-prone affair. A first-time user in Miami broke a leg after launching himself off a bidet that suddenly produced a scalding spritz. In Dallas, a coffee shop with a bidet has its washroom flooded daily by clueless customers. And American tourists in Japan sometimes find themselves stranded on high-tech bidets, unable to turn off the spray yet powerless to move for fear of soaking everything in sight.

The American aversion to bidets began after World War I. During the war, many American soldiers saw bidets for the first time inside French brothels, and the ribald tales they brought back gave bidets a naughty reputation. When the Ritz Hotel in New York decided to put bidets in its bathrooms to appeal to foreign clientele, moral crusaders stirred up such a public outcry that the hotel was forced to remove the "wicked devices."

Though bidets have been associated with licentiousness, they were originally made in the interests of water conservation. In France, where water shortages were a concern, the bidet allowed people to wash intimate areas without having a full bath or shower. Early bidets resembled a small stool with a porcelain or metal basin set in the middle, and were used by both sexes. The first record of the fixture dates from the early eighteenth century when a French Marquis was granted audience by Madame de Prie while she sat on her bidet. Far from scandalous, receiving guests in the bathroom was the height of fashion at the time.

Over the last twenty years, the number of French homes with bidets has dropped by more than half, while the use of bidets has tripled in Japan, now perhaps the world's most bidet-obsessed nation. Alas, in the U.S., it's still more customary to giggle at a bidet than to use it.

## mind the gap

Bidets do not have seats like those found on toilets because any space between a seat and the fixture would allow water to splash out. Sitting directly atop a bidet contains the spray of water.

## ride 'em cowboy

The word "bidet" is derived from the French word meaning "pony" since both are mounted in a similar fashion. It has also been referred to as "the hygienic little horse" in Italy and "the hygienic guitar" in Spain.

## gender bender

The bidet started off as a unisex item, but by the nineteenth century, they fell into disrepute and only were being used discreetly by women. Contrary to popular perception, today's bidets can again be used by both sexes.

## it takes two

In the mid-eighteenth century when socializing in the bathroom was all the rage in France, some well-to-do homeowners installed double bidets that resembled loveseats.

## portable, not potable

Not satisfied with producing home models, several Japanese companies have launched portable bidets. The smallest one can be slipped into a purse or a pant pocket and carries seven fluid ounces of water.

## bomb shelter

In 1762, a portable metal bidet was manufactured for use by officers on the battlefield. The bidet came with a guarantee it could resist the shaking caused by bombardment.

# books and magazines

Surveys show that today as many as six out of ten people read in the bathroom. But six hundred years ago, virtually no one read—anywhere. In Europe in the early 1400s, reading was the preserve of a tiny handful of monks, nobles, and thinkers. The number of people owning books was even smaller. At the time, there was simply no way of producing multiple copies of a book except through costly and time-consuming transcription by hand.

All of this changed in 1455 when row after row of identical Bibles appeared on display at the Frankfurt Trade Fair. Fairgoers were so amazed by the perfect regularity of the calligraphy from book to book that some even suspected, ironically, that the Bibles were the work of the devil. The books, however, were the work of Johann Gutenberg, who altered the course of history by printing the world's first books with movable metal type. His presses churned out three hundred copies of a page a day, making books the first mass-produced item. Printing technology spread, and the number of books produced in the fifty years after the invention of movable type equaled the number produced in the one thousand years before it. Gutenberg's press had a dramatic impact. It led to mass literacy and the widespread dissemination of knowledge; it put religious texts directly into the hands of lay readers, spurring the Reformation; and it catalyzed Europe's industrial and scientific revolutions.

Two centuries after the advent of the printing press, magazines appeared. They began as multipaged pamphlets that bridged the gap between newspapers and books. The earliest magazines were highbrow periodicals, including the German Erbauliche Monaths-Unterredungen (Edifying Monthly Discussions, 1663) and the French Journal des Savants (1665). Less lofty fare appeared by the 1700s, such as magazines devoted to social gossip and women's interests. Magazines have since become a vital part of pop culture—and bathroom culture. They are read more often in the loo than any other material.

## seats of learning

In the United States, National Bathroom Reading Week is celebrated every year in the second week of June.

## face value

*Ladies Home Journal* debuted in Pennsylvania in 1883. Most magazines of the era used the same cover art issue after issue, but *LHJ* daringly changed its cover every month, establishing a key feature of the modern magazine.

## character flaw

Movable type made of clay was invented in China as early as the eleventh century, but the Chinese language's fifty thousand characters made printing impractical. Gutenberg apparently knew nothing of this earlier innovation.

## man overboard

The world's bestselling women's magazine is *Cosmopolitan*, but when it began in New York in 1886, it was a pseudo-anthropological journal with the non-inclusive motto "The world is my country and all mankind are my countrymen." Girl power took over at *Cosmo* in 1965.

## degrees of separation

Who reads in the bathroom? According to a survey by Scott Paper, 50 percent of those with a high school education, 56 percent of those with bachelor's degrees, and over two-thirds of those with advanced degrees.

## babel-ing on

The world's all-time bestselling author is likely William Shakespeare. By most accounts, the bestselling book ever is the Bible, which has been printed in more than eight hundred languages.

# cleaning products

As much as we love our bathrooms, cleaning them is always an unenviable task. In the late 1800s, those who could afford to have fully outfitted bathrooms also could afford to hire servants to scrub and scour. But as the middle class swelled during the twentieth century, more and more people found themselves able to pay for modern bathroom fixtures but not hired help. As a result, cleaning the bathroom became a bit of household drudgery taken up by millions—especially women—which in turn created a ready market for cleaning products.

The first commercially successful cleaning product, Bon Ami (French for "good friend"), debuted in Connecticut in 1886. It was created by setting feldspar powder into bars of soap. The feldspar gave the soap a gentle abrasive quality, and Bon Ami remained a top seller even through the Depression. Soap-based cleaners, however, were slowly muscled out by detergents through the 1930s and '40s. Developed by the Germans during World War I, detergents cleaned without producing the scum that soap left behind.

The demand for cleaning agents soared after World War II as populations boomed and suburbs sprawled. In 1946, the Colgate-Palmolive Company launched a scouring powder named after a warrior from Greek mythology: Ajax. It remained a runaway bestseller for a decade, but in 1957 Proctor & Gamble introduced Comet with a well-funded ad campaign. Comet, touted as gentler on porcelain surfaces, quickly matched Ajax in popularity, and the two brands have been battling each other for bathroom-cleaner supremacy ever since.

In the 1970s, Comet ads featuring an "all-knowing" male voice explaining to a woman how to clean a bathroom were criticized by women's groups as chauvinistic. The women's groups had a point: a recent survey has shown that 87 percent of Americans learned to clean from their mothers, while 63 percent learned ways to avoid housework from their fathers.

## once in a lifetime offer

In 1986, Proctor & Gamble capitalized on the fuss over the return of Haley's Comet by printing one million "Haley's Comet" booklets that were given away with the purchase of P & G's Comet cleanser.

## the king and I

Mr. Clean all-purpose cleanser was launched in 1959. The muscular cartoon Mr. Clean was loosely modeled after Yul Brynner, an American actor, and Djinn, the genie from Aladdin's Lamp.

## in hot water

Drāno drain opener, introduced in 1923, contains the caustic cleaning agent lye. When dissolved in water, lye releases large amounts of heat which literally melt away grease and grime.

## going dutch

The phrase "spic and span" derives from the Dutch term *spiksplinternieuw,* used to describe ships with new spikes and splinters. The term was anglicized to "spick and spannew," and then to "spic and span." The cleaner by the same name debuted in 1933.

## sol-ved

Lysol was first imported to the U.S. from Germany in the 1870s, while Pine-Sol was created in Mississippi in 1929. The brand names are short for "lye solvent" and "pine solvent," respectively.

## bad case of gas

During World War II, chlorine bleach was used as a decontaminant for poison gas. Clorox even ran ads in the United States on how to use their bleach in the event of a poison gas attack.

# cold medicines

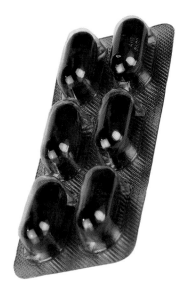

Chinese legend has it that in the fourth millennium B.C., the Emperor Shen Nung resolved to try various plants each day in order to discover their medicinal qualities. In the process, he poisoned himself one hundred times, which forced him to find one hundred corresponding cures. While this story may be sheer fiction, what is certainly true is that pharmacy began as a process of trial and error. Over thousands of years, the ancients experimented with various remedies and passed down their knowledge of anything that worked. By 3500 B.C., the Sumerians had developed almost all modern methods of administering drugs, including pills, lotions, gargles, decoctions, inhalations, suppositories, and enemas. The first pharmacopoeia (drug catalogue), written by a Sumerian doctor, listed cures for cold symptoms. Salt dissolved in water was prescribed for sore throats, while crushed willow bark was suggested for fever. In 1000 B.C., the Egyptians created the first cough drops with herbs and honey.

The manufacturing of medicine remained a folk art for centuries. It wasn't until the 1600s that the first medication was patented in England. However, many medicine-makers avoided patents since ingredients had to be fully disclosed. Unique brand names were trademarked instead so that nostrums could be legally protected—contents unspecified. This lead to a boom in "cure-all" elixirs of dubious merit. In the 1800s, many cold remedies contained high amounts of alcohol. Some contained addictive drugs such as opium and cocaine, while others had no active ingredients at all. Governments eventually stepped in to curb the fraud. Today, legitimate patent medicines are in homes everywhere, including Tylenol (1955), the first widely used acetaminophen-based analgesic; Dristan (1957), the first multi-symptom cold remedy; and Contac (1961), the first "time-release" medication.

By the way, it never hurts to keep medicine cabinets well-stocked—the average person suffers up to two hundred colds in a lifetime.

## globetrotting

A century ago, it took about four months for a particular strain of the flu to circle the globe. With the advent of air travel, a flu virus can now circle the planet in four days.

### avian water

Scientific studies show that the most popular cold remedy not found in the medicine chest, chicken soup, does relieve cold symptoms. Plain chicken broth, however, won't do the job. Only chicken soup made with veggies proved to be effective.

### namesake

Vapor rubs used to treat head colds contain menthol, an ingredient first popularized in 1898 by a sore-muscle balm called Ben-Gay. It was named after its inventor, French pharmacist Jules Bengué.

### all in the family

In the early 1900s, both morphine and heroin (a morphine derivative) were popular cough suppressants. Today, a much weaker morphine derivative, codeine, is still used to treat serious coughs.

### tough lesson

Tamper-resistant packaging became a drug-industry standard after seven people died in 1982 from Tylenol capsules tainted with cyanide. Tylenol launched new packaging with three different protective seals, and was able to win back consumer confidence.

### with a little help from my friends

Studies have shown that people with large groups of friends are four times less likely to get sick compared with people with just a few friends. This may be because people with many friends are happier, which can give the immune system a boost.

# cologne

Men and fragrance go back a long way. Some believe perfume was introduced to the world ten thousand years ago by a man—the Yellow Emperor of China. When King Tutankhamen died in 1352 B.C., he was buried alongside bottles of perfume to ensure he would smell sweet in the afterlife. And in the tenth century B.C., Solomon, a man of legendary libido, charmed his seven hundred wives and three hundred concubines by wearing fragrances. But despite this storied past, it wasn't until the eighteenth century that the greatest male scent of all time was born: cologne.

In 1709, Italian barber Gian Paolo Feminis headed to Cologne, Germany, to seek his fortune. He soon began selling a perfume scented with grape spirits, bergamot, lavender, and lemon. Public response to his "water" was so enthusiastic, he enlisted his nephew, Giovanni Maria Farina, to help run the business. As sales boomed, so did copy-cats. Scores of perfume-makers began masquerading as members of the Farina clan, forcing the real Farina to wage legal battles with imposters for years. In the mid-1700s, French soldiers stationed in Cologne dubbed the new scent eau de cologne and brought it back to France, where it was a huge hit among men and women alike. Farina peddled eau de cologne as a cure-all that was not only good for the skin, but for the stomach as well—it was drunk as a tonic. Not content to cure human ails, Farina even recommended cologne for animals.

For much of the nineteenth and twentieth centuries, it was considered unmanly to wear fragrances. But this changed during World War II when the makers of Old Spice aftershave convinced the U.S. Army to put their product into soldiers' standard-issue toiletry kits. The promotion helped give aftershave and cologne a new macho image, and today men's products comprise one-third of the lucrative perfume market. Though eau de cologne was and still is worn by both sexes, the word "cologne" has nevertheless become synonymous with the well-scented man.

## lying down on the job

Napoleon's favorite fragrance was eau de cologne. He used several bottles a day, likely to counter Josephine's favorite scent, musk, which he hated. The Empress wore so much musk that servants in her over-perfumed boudoir often fainted.

## good for the fellas

The film credits of famed American director Martin Scorcese include *Mean Streets, Taxi Driver, Raging Bull*, and a commercial for the fragrance Armani pour Homme.

## feline fetor

Literary references to men's fragrances include Shakespeare's mention of civet-scented dandies. Civet is a pasty white secretion scraped from the anal glands of the wild civet cat, and has a horrid fecal odor unless diluted and mixed with other essences.

## made to measure

In the perfume trade, eau de cologne has a general meaning as a measure of dilution, referring to fragrances with 3 to 5 percent essential oils. Eau de toilette contains 5 to 12 percent, eau de parfum uses 12 to 18 percent, while true perfumes have 18 percent or more.

## calamary calamity

Ambergris, derived from sperm whales, is a fixative that extends the life of a fragrance. It forms when a whale eats a giant squid, which has indigestible bones. When the whale's intestines become irritated, ambergris is secreted as a protective reaction.

## wild about it

Eau Sauvage, launched by Christian Dior in 1956, was the first men's fragrance that dared to use floral scents. It was as popular among women as men, and sparked a fashion for unisex fragrances.

# combs

Anthropologists believe that almost all early peoples independently invented combs, with one notable exception: the Britons. Content to endure an endless string of bad hair days, Britons didn't begin combing their hair until 789 A.D. when the Danes first invaded and brought with them a taste for grooming. This is all the more bewildering considering the earliest known combs date back to the Stone Age (10 to 15,000 B.C.). The very first combs were made of wood, ivory, and fish bones. They weren't used to create swanky hairdos, but to remove insects, lice, and dirt from the head. With the advent of metal tools, harder materials such as horn, baleen, walrus, alabaster, onyx, ebony, and boxwood also were carved into combs. From culture to culture, early combs looked strikingly similar, and combs with five or ten teeth suggest that they may have been modeled after human hands.

The ancient Egyptians were likely the first to produce double-sided combs with coarse and fine rows of teeth set on opposite sides. This design became standard in both European and Asian cultures for centuries. The fine side was probably used for cleaning, while the coarse side was used to style and separate hair. For some reason, the idea of having graduated teeth on just one side of a comb did not catch on until the nineteenth century.

Combs were first made in the United States in the late 1700s when New England farmers turned to comb-making during the winter months for extra income. But at the time, tortoise shell combs from China remained the most prized. Even during a period of Chinese cultural isolation in the eighteenth century, one street in the city of Canton remained open for trade with foreign buyers, and their shopping lists always included combs. The advent of plastic in the 1930s, however, ultimately spelled the demise of exotic materials. Today, cheap and flimsy combs sit in bathrooms, purses, and pockets everywhere—even in Britain.

## stop, drop, and roll

Celluloid, an early form of plastic, was used to make combs in the late 1800s. However, celluloid combs were soon banned from the market since they were highly flammable.

### the midas touch

The most valuable comb in the world was found in the tomb of a Scythian leader near the steppes of the Black Sea. Dating from the fifth century B.C., the comb is made of over ten ounces of pure gold.

### cyrillic seduction

One of the world's most celebrated combs was carved in eastern Siberia during the eighteenth century out of ivory from the extinct wooly mammoth. The comb sports a Russian inscription which reads, "I present it to him whom I love."

### beauty pageant

Before the nineteenth century, hair ornaments and decorative combs were the most important kinds of jewelry in China and Japan. Well-to-do Japanese women even competed to see who could wear the most combs.

### mis-lead

Europeans in the sixteenth century believed that gray hairs could be fought off by stroking tresses with a lead comb. While microscopic flakes of black lead from a comb could have darkened hair, there's no hard evidence lead combs really worked.

### going over her head

There are two main types of combs: utilitarian dressing combs and decorative combs (which include some tiaras). Queen Victoria is said to have preferred tiaras and simpler crowns since her five pound Imperial State Crown "hurt her a great deal."

# contact lenses

Vanity, vanity, all is vanity. If humans didn't have such a narcissistic streak, contact lenses might have remained a bizarre footnote in medical history. As it turned out, people were more than willing to stick painful foreign objects into their eyes in the name of beauty.

Early contact lenses were hard to make and even harder to wear. Users were fitted for contacts through a torturous process of trial and error with various-sized lenses or by having wax poured over their eyes to create molds. The first lenses were so large they even covered the whites of the eyes, cutting off tear flow. Since eyes dried quickly, contacts could only be tolerated for an hour or two. Lenses were made of glass and broke easily. They were also corroded by body acids, which made the glass surfaces rough and highly irritating. Early prototypes were so clumsy, in fact, that some could only be worn with a topical anesthetic. August Müller, one of three European scientists who independently developed contact lenses around 1888, recommended an anesthetic solution of cocaine.

The introduction of plastic in the 1930s was a great leap forward for contact lenses. Plastic lenses rarely broke and were inert to body acids, but as with glass lenses, vision still became hazy after a few hours. Clinicians tried to reduce the cloudiness by perforating or scoring lenses to improve tear flow. The problem was not solved, however, until corneal lenses were launched in the 1950s. Instead of covering the entire eye, these ultra-light lenses floated on a layer of tears over just the cornea. This greatly improved comfort and wearing time. Another landmark was reached in 1959 when Czech chemists invented a water-absorbing plastic that proved ideal for soft lenses. From 1950 to 1980, contact lenses slowly evolved from a medical curio into an everyday accessory. Wearing contact lenses, once the height of folly, is now just another taken-for-granted routine of the twenty-first century.

## a fine vintage

1987 was an auspicious year for contact lenses. Both disposable contact lenses and colored contact lenses were introduced in this year.

## power surge

Czech scientist Otto Wichterle helped invent the soft contact lens. In the 1960s, he made lenses in his kitchen with a makeshift machine that included part of a bicycle generator. To produce power, Wichterle and his wife took turns pedaling.

## salty and sweet

Most of today's contact lens solutions have a saline formula. However, the very first doctor-recommended solution, proposed by Swiss contact lens pioneer Adolph Eugene Fick in 1888, was a 2 percent solution of grape sugar.

## dead set

The very first clinical trials of contact lenses were conducted on rabbits. The very first contact lenses for humans were made from plaster molds set from cadaver eyes.

## seeing the light

Scientists in Germany are working on contact lenses that will not only correct ordinary vision problems, but also will provide a five-fold improvement in night vision. This would make our nighttime sight better than that of owls or cats.

## bad credit

Leonardo da Vinci is often credited with inventing the contact lens in 1508, but his notes and sketches describe a crude forerunner at best. The first suggestion of contact lenses as we know them today is more properly credited to British astronomer Sir John F. W. Herschel, who made mention of them in 1827.

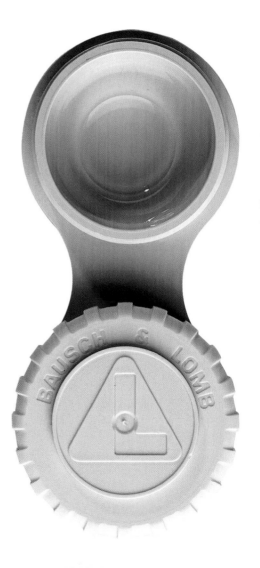

# cotton swabs

U.S. President Woodrow Wilson once remarked, "Originality is simply a fresh pair of eyes." Polish-born American Leo Gerstenzang certainly would have agreed since a fresh pair of eyes is precisely what led him to his idea for cotton swabs. One day in 1923 while watching his wife bathe their new-born, Gerstenzang noticed her wrapping a wad of cotton around the end of a toothpick. His wife then used the makeshift device to clean the baby's ears and other hard-to-reach spots. Unfortunately, preparing the swab while holding a fidgety baby was no easy feat. Gerstenzang quickly realized that a ready-made cotton swab might be a handy baby accessory—and a potential gold mine. Being mechanically inclined, he set about building a machine that could churn out ready-to-use cotton swabs.

Gerstenzang wanted his new swab to be foolproof. He knew if wooden sticks splintered or cotton ends fell off, baby injuries—and lawsuits—would quickly mount. After several years of tinkering, Gerstenzang perfected a machine in 1925 that produced safe and reliable swabs. The machine also packaged the swabs in a sliding tray box designed to be easily opened with one hand. Each box was then sterilized and sealed with transparent wrapping. Since production was entirely automated, the phrase "untouched by human hands" later became a popular marketing mantra for Gerstenzang's invention.

No doubt convinced of the joy he would bring to babies all around the world, Gerstenzang named his new product Baby Gays. In 1926, the name was changed to Q-Tips Baby Gays, and eventually to just Q-Tips. The name change was apropos since people have found countless uses for cotton swabs besides baby care. Q-Tips was the only product of its kind available to consumers until 1941. Since then, other cotton swab brands have muscled in on the market, but Q-Tips safely remains the granddaddy of them all.

## hot to trot

American pop artist Andy Warhol once divulged, "One of the things that gets me hot is having a Q-Tip in my ear."

### not quantity

Here's the answer to your burning question: the "Q" in Q-Tips stands for "quality."

### be all ears

It is safe to clean around the rim of the ear with a cotton swab, but swabs should never be stuck inside the ear canal. Doing this can not only damage the delicate eardrum, but can actually push earwax deeper into the ear.

### cotton is king

Cotton is the most important non-food agricultural commodity in the world. The earliest evidence of human-made cotton materials have been found in tombs in India, and date as far back as 3500 B.C.

### sticky situation

In 1958, Q-Tips, Inc., bought machinery from a British company called Papersticks Ltd. The machinery, used to make lollipop sticks, was adapted to produce paper sticks for swabs. Today, Q-Tips boasts their sticks are "biodegradable when composted."

### fleshing things out

Cotton swabs have hundreds of uses beyond baby care. They are used by restorationists to clean artwork, by law-enforcement agents to collect explosive traces, and by beauticians to apply makeup. When Chairman Mao died in 1976, his body was prepared for public display with the help of flesh-colored makeup and cotton swabs.

# dental floss

Cleaning food out from between our teeth is one of humankind's oldest habits. The practice is so old, in fact, we were barely human when we started—fossil evidence shows that our half-erect ancestors were using toothpicks 1.8 million years ago. By the time civilization emerged, tooth-picking was in full swing. Toothpicks were so prized that the Babylonians buried them with the dead, while the Chinese wore them as pendants. The latter custom was taken up by Europeans during the Renaissance; those who could pay for the privilege wore gold toothpicks around their necks and wielded them with great pomp after meals.

Not content with the cleaning power of the venerable toothpick, dentist Levi Spear Parmly built a better mousetrap in 1819: dental floss. Parmly, who practiced in France, England, Canada, and the United States, advocated the use of waxed silk thread to remove lodged food. He was so zealous in his crusade for oral hygiene that he would stop complete strangers in public, inspect their teeth, and school them on the correct methods of flossing.

When silk became unavailable during World War II, another oral hygiene fanatic, Charles C. Bass of Mississippi, pioneered the use of nylon dental floss. He stubbornly insisted there was only one effective way to maintain oral hygiene—his way. The Bass Method specified that the "right kind" of floss was made of unwaxed nylon yarn which was composed of 170 loosely wound filaments. He produced this floss himself but refused to profit from his creation. Bass sold his floss at wholesale prices and only to dentists willing to visit his office, where he would personally demonstrate the correct flossing technique. For years, the cantankerous Bass railed against the dental profession for failing to promote oral hygiene in the home. According to the latest figures, there's still plenty of work to be done—only one in four people in industrialized countries flosses regularly.

## coming up short

If we followed dentists' orders and used a foot-and-a-half of dental floss every day, each person would be buying 183 yards a year. The actual amount bought by each person, however, averages only 18 yards.

## the great escape

In 1991, three prisoners in Texas planned to escape with a ladder made of braided dental floss, but were foiled before they got the chance. Three years later, an inmate in West Virginia scaled a wall with a dental floss rope and got away.

## heart-warning news

Not only does flossing help prevent tooth decay, it can even help reduce the risk of premature death. Some scientists think flossing removes bacteria that might otherwise migrate into the bloodstream and cause blood clots, potentially triggering heart attacks and strokes.

## stuck in the middle

A piece of shredded floss lodged between two teeth is sometimes excruciatingly painful. This is because the floss can expand and actually push your teeth apart.

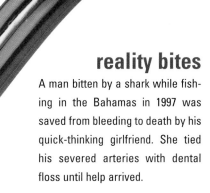

## reality bites

A man bitten by a shark while fishing in the Bahamas in 1997 was saved from bleeding to death by his quick-thinking girlfriend. She tied his severed arteries with dental floss until help arrived.

## sew-sew ideas

Since the tensile strength of dental floss is superior to most commercial threads, outdoorsy folks use floss for everything from reinforcing buttons to patching up tents.

# deodorant

Having body odor can be a mortifying experience, but medical research has found that exuding an underarm stench can downright ruin your life. Studies show that people with foul body odors suffer problems with relationships, diminished prospects of promotion at work, underachievement in school because of bullying, and feelings of embarrassment and shame. No wonder billions of dollars worth of deodorants are scooped up every year. Deodorants work by killing the smell-producing bacteria that thrive off otherwise odorless secretions from our apocrine glands—a type of sweat gland concentrated in a tennis ball-sized patch in our armpits. Oddly, most Asians have few or no apocrine glands. In Japan, 90 percent of the population has no discernable underarm smell, but at one time, the hapless men who did could even be dismissed from the military on that ground alone.

The bid to snuff out B.O. began thousands of years ago when the Egyptians created perfumed citrus and cinnamon lotions that were smeared under the arms. In Europe, myrtle oil and other floral perfumes were used to mask smells for centuries, and by the 1700s, animal scents such as musk also became popular odor-fighters. However, nothing kills a stench like a good bath, and most Europeans simply didn't take enough of them, if any.

The first commercial deodorant, Mum, was launched in 1888. It contained bacteria-killing zinc oxide that silenced smells, but the heyday of deodorants didn't begin until after World War II. Greater disposable incomes, faith in modern science, and slick marketing all contributed to the deodorant boom and our current obsession with stink-free bodies. Early creams and sprays were messy, but technology borrowed from ball-point pens gave rise to the first roll-on deodorant in 1955. Now we can also buy sticks, gels, and improved sprays, giving us plenty of weapons to ensure our underarms aren't foul—and our lives aren't fouled up.

## scents of self

Several studies have shown that people are able to pick out their own and their spouses' undershirts (worn for a week) from others' by smell.

## getting their act together

Women who live together know that their menstrual cycles may synchronize. Some researchers believe this is caused by underarm odors, which influence the secretion of hormones from the pituitary gland, which may in turn regulate menstruation.

## continental divide

The biggest deodorant market in the world is the U.S., followed by Germany, France, Italy, and Spain. North Americans prefer roll-on and stick deodorants, while Europeans are more likely to fight B.O. with a spray.

## fetching pheromones

Albert Einstein is said to have been more attracted to women "the more they smelled." Napoleon once wrote to his lover Josephine, "I will be arriving in Paris tomorrow evening. Don't wash."

## old-fashioned olfaction

Many large deodorant manufacturers test the effectiveness of their new products in an uncomplicated way—they employ people to sniff others' armpits.

## mincing words

In the mid-1900s, body odor was still a taboo subject. Colgate furtively peddled deodorants by claiming its "Veto" brand could ensure "your own exquisite daintiness," while its "Fresh" brand made women "lovelier to love."

# diapers

A baby's need to "go to the bathroom" was a trifling concern for our tribal ancestors. Women carried babies in slings or swaddles, and could easily recognize the cues—altered facial expressions, stomach gurgling, and fidgety behavior—that nature was calling. The infant would then be "held out" to do his or her duty. But as humans became less nomadic, primitive diapers came into use. Far-flung peoples from Native Americans to the Romans all used simple, natural materials for diapers such as milkweed leaves, moss, or animal skins. From ancient times until the twentieth century, diaper technology saw little change.

Diapers in the early 1900s were mostly rectangular pieces of cotton, folded around a baby's bottom and held in place with pins. The thankless job of changing, washing, boiling, and folding diapers, of course, fell to women. But during World War II, women busy building tanks and bombs were often too exhausted to wash diapers. Before long, diaper services began springing up to help give moms a break. The services, however, tended to be expensive, and no matter who did the washing, folded diapers still leaked.

Fed up with reusables, American Marion Donovan used absorbent padding and a piece of shower curtain to create a disposable diaper called the Boater in 1951. Despite rave reviews for the Boater, by the late 1950s, disposables still accounted for less than 1 percent of diaper changes in the U.S. But a new era of baby care was ushered in with the launch of Pampers in 1961. Pampers almost single-handedly created the U.S. market for disposables by being reliable yet cheap enough for everyday use. It hit international markets in the 1970s. Rival brand Huggies debuted in 1977, sparking a "features war" between the two brands that brought diaper innovations such as elasticized legs, refastenable tapes, and superabsorbent filling. Even with these advances, diaper-changing remains a Herculean task. Parents need to change a baby eight to twelve times a day, or over ten thousand times in total.

## powder keg

Talcum powder has been a part of diaper changes for over a century. Johnson's Baby Powder debuted in 1893, and has been packaged in its trademark white plastic container since 1963.

## name dropping

Before Proctor & Gamble decided on Pampers, they considered and rejected other names for their diapers, including Zephyrs, Larks, Tads, Winks, Solos, and Dri-Wees.

## strange bedfellows

Diaper machines work at lightning speed, some churning out more than eight hundred diapers a minute. Since Pampers uses the same statistical methods to predict production reliability as arms makers, it has been working to improve diaper production with the Los Alamos National Laboratory, a nuclear weapons research facility.

## clogged arteries

Some early disposable diapers sold in the 1960s were advertised as "flushable." Predictably, they clogged drain pipes, quickly negating the benefits of using throw-aways.

## lost love

Disposable diapers were not always an easy sell in the 1960s. Mothers felt their love for their babies was reflected by the time spent attending to them. Using disposables left some women racked with guilt since they were spending less time on baby care.

## keeping the homes fires from burning

Firefighters can protect homes from encroaching fires by spraying them with a water-absorbing gel. The gel contains sodium polyacrylate, the same super-absorbent polymer used in disposable diapers.

# electric razors

The story of the electric razor begins in a gold-mining camp in the nether regions of Alaska. Jacob Schick, a retired U.S. Army lieutenant, went to the camp in 1910 on medical advice that the frigid Alaskan climate would keep his recurring dysentery in check. While the sub-zero weather was a boon to his bowels, it was a handicap when it came to shaving. Melting snow into water for a morning shave was an annoying ritual. Even if Schick had water saved up, he couldn't get to it until he cracked open the layer of ice that would form on top. Since Schick had a military pedigree, giving up his morning shave was out of the question. Instead, he took it upon himself to invent a method of shaving without water.

After one final military stint during World War I, Schick retired for good in 1919 as a colonel and returned to his pet project of creating a "dry" electric shaver. At the time, powerful motors were still big and bulky. Schick worked for years to create smaller ones, and patented his first electric shaver in 1923. However, the design was impractical since one hand was needed to hold the motor, the other to hold the cutting head. While Schick worked on improvements, he launched an ingenious wet razor in 1926—the Magazine Repeating Razor. Based on the repeating army rifle, the razor featured a mechanism that dispensed and ejected blades automatically. But Schick kept tinkering with the electric razor, and in 1928 he finally came up with a much-improved design. Betting the world was ready for a shaving revolution, he sold his wet razor company and mortgaged his home to finance his dream.

In 1931, smack in the middle of the Depression, Schick put his electric shaver on the market. With a hefty price tag of $25, first-year sales were underwhelming—only three thousand were sold. With heavy advertising, though, two million electric shavers were bought by 1937, and the battle between wet-shave and dry-shave loyalists has raged ever since.

## dull razors

According to a Schick survey, over 95 percent of men who shave find it boring.

## border skirmish

Jacob Schick, the inventor of the electric razor and one-time Colonel in the U.S. Army, renounced his U.S. citizenship in 1935 to move to Canada. President Roosevelt was livid, calling Schick a tax-dodger. Schick explained that Canada's cold weather would improve his health, but he died after only eighteen months.

## cutting edge technology

Engineer Alexandre Horowitz created many products for the Philips Company of the Netherlands, including the world's first double-headed electric shaver. During his illustrious career, he received 136 patents for his shaving innovations.

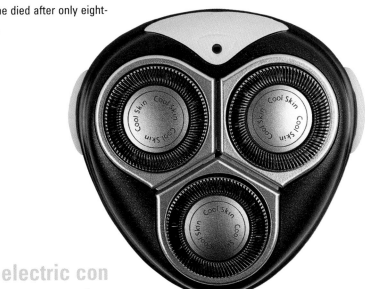

## electric con

Many men claim that a wet shave with a blade simply "feels better." Here's the reason why: electric razors do not exfoliate dead skin. A wet shave does, leaving a man's face feeling smoother and fresher.

## doing it in public

In the 1950s, men on the run had the option of shaving in public with coin-operated electric razors.

## electric pro

Razor blades cut at an angle and leave hairs with a sharp point. For curly-haired men, angled hair stumps can curl back into the skin and cause irritations. Electric razors cut hairs straight across and flush with the skin, solving the problem.

# eye makeup

In the late nineteenth century, makeup in the West was passé. In England, where social censure against cosmetics was unusually harsh, the only women who wore makeup in the day were prostitutes. But "respectable" ladies did sometimes create their own cosmetics for evening. Eyeshadow was made from the residue of burnt corks or frankincense, while crude mascara was whipped up with diluted India ink or charred matchsticks.

In the twentieth century, views on makeup began to change. Women were slowly freed from the repressive mores of the 1800s, and a wave of orientalism swept through the West that gave makeup new life. In 1911, Vogue reported that Turkish women colored their eyes with henna, while Arab women used black powder. At the same time, the Russian Ballet was touring Europe, exposing audiences to stylized ballet makeup that made eyes look oblique and elongated. Hollywood also gave eye makeup a boost. In the Roaring Twenties, Max Factor dabbed hot black wax onto the lashes of Clara Bow, and by 1929, Greta Garbo (worshipped for her long lashes) was the biggest attraction on the silver screen.

In the mid-1900s, mascara was mostly made with beeswax, carbauna wax, and water. The best-selling mascara of all time, Maybelline's Great Lash Mascara, debuted in 1971. Today, it still sells at the remarkable clip of one every 1.9 seconds.

Though eye makeup is more popular now than ever, its history stretches back over ten thousand years. The early Egyptians lined their eyes with green malachite and black kohl, both to beautify and to protect eyes from glare. These ancient cosmetics were surprisingly sophisticated. Scientists have found that Egyptian eye makeup had expiration dates, and was thickened with 7 to 10 percent fat—the same proportion used in most eye makeup today.

## unionist sympathies

The ancient Romans darkened their eyebrows with antimony, lead, or soot, and considered eyebrows that joined together over the nose a mark of great beauty.

## sex change

In 1926, Frenchman Edouard Pinaud launched Mascara 612, which contained sticky plant gums. The mascara was inspired by a men's product—the Hungarian ointment Napoleon III used to groom his mustache.

## by the book

A powder called *mesdjem*, which was used as early as 3000 B.C. to improve the growth of eyelashes, is referred to in the Koran. A recipe for mascara is given in the ancient erotic Sanskrit text the *Kama Sutra*.

## working wonders

Lash-curling mascaras contain elastic polymers that shrink as they dry, causing eyelashes to arch upward. When Maybelline launched Wonder Curl mascara in Japan in 1999 (Asian lashes usually grow straight), its mascara sales jumped from one million units a year to over one million units a month.

## eyebrow-razing facts

From the mid-1800s up to the 1930s, some fashionable women who were unhappy with their eyebrows shaved them off and glued on replacements instead. One popular material for faux eyebrows was mouse fur.

## brotherly love

After nineteen-year-old American T.L. Williams saw his sister Mabel moisten her eyelashes with petroleum jelly in 1915, he was inspired to create a line of eye cosmetics. In honor of his sister, he called his company Maybelline.

# facial tissue

The story of facial tissue is the story of Kleenex. Though the Kimberly-Clark Corporation of Neenah, Wisconsin, produces the only true Kleenex, the brand name has been used as a colloquial term for facial tissue for decades. Kleenex was introduced in 1924, but its origins go back a decade earlier. During World War I when supplies of cotton dwindled, Kimberly-Clark scientists developed a highly absorbent substitute: Cellucotton. This cellulose wadding came to the rescue of hospitals and first aid stations that had run out of cotton bandages. Anticipating huge demand, Kimberly-Clark manufactured reams of Cellucotton. The war's end, however, left the company with mountains of surplus tissue.

Kimberly-Clark looked for ways to peddle the leftover material. Hoping to distance Cellucotton from its wartime image, the company decided to market the tissue as a glam product: a disposable towel to remove makeup. It was christened Kleenex, and one hundred sheets sold for sixty-five cents—pricey by 1924 standards. Despite glowing Hollywood endorsements, sales were tame. Many who did buy Kleenex, however, wrote to say they loved using the tissues to blow their noses.

Perplexed, the company conducted a poll in 1930. It ran two different newspaper ads in Peoria, Illinois. One headline read: "There is no way like Kleenex to remove cold cream." The other read: "Kleenex is wonderful for handkerchiefs." Each ad included a coupon, which doubled as a ballot, promising the redeemer a free box of Kleenex. When the votes were tallied, the results were clear: 61 percent of those polled used Kleenex as a throwaway hankie. Kimberly-Clark quickly revamped its ads. Pitching the slogan, "Don't put a cold in your pocket," the company quadrupled Kleenex sales in two years, and the rest is history. Today, Kleenex is everywhere—not only taking its rightful place in our homes, but in our dictionaries as well.

## pop quiz

How many boxes of tissue does the average American use every year? Answer: 8.3

## easy access

The pop-up tissue box, which holds tissues in interfolded layers, was developed by Chicago inventor Andrew Olson in 1929. The first Kleenex tissues sold in pop-up boxes were marketed as "Serv-a-Tissue."

## fateful decision

Kimberly-Clark, the famed manufacturer of Kleenex, was named after two of the four founding partners. If it had been named after the other two, it would have been the far less mellifluous sounding Babcock-Shattuck.

## neat freak

American industrialist, aviator, and filmmaker Howard Hughes became so neurotic about germs in his later life that he had his floors covered with Kleenex before receiving guests. After people walked on the Kleenex, he had the tissues thrown out.

## life saver

A thicker, more absorbent version of Cellucotton (the original material used for making Kleenex) was used as a gas-mask filter towards the end of World War I.

## final answer

In the 1940s, the cartoon character Little Lulu began appearing in Kleenex ads. Lulu's creator, Margaret Buell, was already drawing the cartoon for the *Saturday Evening Post* at the time. While the *Post* gave permission for Lulu to appear in Kleenex ads, it later gave Ms. Buell an ultimatum: choose one job or the other. She chose Kleenex.

# false teeth

For most of human history, replacing missing teeth has been a sad and sorry cause. Finding teeth has always been easy enough—animal teeth, artificial teeth, dead people's teeth—but getting them to stay in during dinner was another story. The Etruscans did develop reliable gold bridgework as early as 700 B.C., but their craft vanished along with the Roman Empire. During the ensuing Dark Ages, teeth were often pulled but rarely replaced.

Dental prosthetics were available to the rich in Europe by the 1600s, but problems abounded. False teeth tied to their natural neighbors with silk threads were clumsy and uncomfortable. Dentures made with human teeth set in hippopotamus ivory soon rotted, giving off a horrific stench and releasing toxins. Upper dentures also fell down, prompting some fashion-conscious Parisians to hang dentures from their gums with hooks. The problem of gravity was solved by pushing the upper and lower dentures apart with steel springs, but constant pressure was now needed to keep the mouth shut. Disconcertingly, the set of teeth could also spring out of the wearer's mouth without warning.

In 1774, the French duo of Duchateau and de Chemant introduced an "incorruptible" denture made of porcelain. Though ill-fitting, fragile, and expensive, it did spark further research into inorganic dentures. However, "Waterloo teeth"—teeth collected from the corpses of young soldiers in the aftermath of war—remained widely preferred. It wasn't until the Goodyear brothers developed Vulcanite (hard rubber) in the mid-1800s that an affordable inorganic material for dentures became available. The timing was fortuitous; the advent of painless tooth removal with anesthesia a few years earlier had sent the demand for extractions skyrocketing. Rubber dentures ruled until the rubber shortage of World War II forced dentists to turn to plastic, the material most commonly used today.

## a grave profession

The American Civil War proved to be a windfall for tooth peddlers. They shipped teeth from the war dead to England by the barrel.

52

### leap of faith

The patron saint of dentistry and those afflicted with toothache is St. Apollonia. In the third century A.D., the Romans tortured her by ripping out all of her teeth and threatening to burn her alive. Told to recite blasphemy, she chose instead to leap into the pyre.

### sucking up

Sixteenth century Japanese dentures made of wood were the first full upper dentures to employ suction as a means of retention. This idea was not seen in the West for another two hundred years.

### presidential adversary

Trying to hide their rank odor and taste, George Washington soaked his dentures nightly in port. He was so shamed by the sad state of his teeth, he cut down on speaking engagements.

### jolly interesting

It is theorized that the characteristic dry wit of the English developed in response to the social embarrassment caused by early dentures. Droll humor allowed people to tell jokes without laughing out loud and exposing their putrid dentures.

### a job too well done

After the Goodyear Dental Company obtained a patent for Vulcanite dentures, Josiah Bacon was assigned to sue dentists for patent infringement. Bacon was so zealous in his pursuit of damages that he was finally shot dead by a despondent dentist who was being sued for the third time.

# feminine protection

Menstruation is depicted in cave paintings from the Stone Age, and women's attempts to stay "fresh" and "carefree" likely date back just as far. The world's oldest-known medical document, the Ebers scroll, records that Egyptian women of the fifteenth century b.c. used tampons made of soft papyrus. The early Romans preferred wool, while the Japanese used paper. In Africa, bandages made of plant fibers were favored. Though feminine protection was certainly crude, fertility for ancient women wasn't all bad. Some scholars think pre-industrial women only went through menses 160 times over their lifetimes compared with 450 times for modern women. This is because ancient women began menstruating at a later age, were pregnant more often, and breastfed for longer periods between pregnancies.

In the early 1900s, many women used linen cloths that they washed and reused, which gave rise to the saying, "Don't air your dirty linen in public." A disposable napkin was put on the American market as early as 1896, but sales flopped since most stores were too afraid to advertise the product. It wasn't until the 1920s that the first commercial sanitary napkin was successfully introduced. Kotex brand pads were created after French nurses discovered during World War I that Cellucotton—the material later used to make Kleenex—could be adapted for menstrual use. Kotex pads were bulky, caused chafing, and had to be pinned to undergarments, but they soon made reusable linens virtually obsolete.

## german determined

In 1950, a European subsidiary of Johnson & Johnson launched o.b. brand tampons. "o.b." stands for the German *ohne binde*, meaning "without napkin."

The modern age of feminine protection began when Denver physician Earle Haas reinvented the tampon in 1931. He sold his invention to Tampax five years later. Despite moral objections to tampon use, Tampax soon advertised its way into the hearts of millions with slogans such as "Welcome this new day for womanhood" and "No belts. No pins. No pads." Today, women in search of "freedom" and "confidence" use as many as eleven thousand tampons during their procreative years.

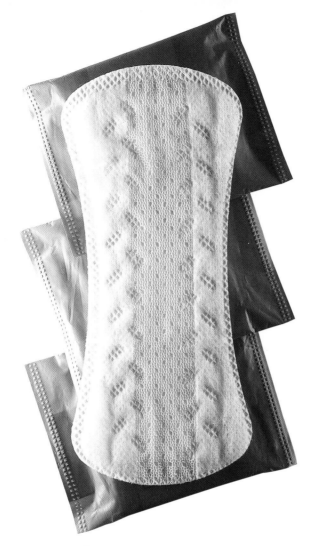

## media blackout

Menstruation was a taboo subject for much of the twentieth century—TV and radio ads for feminine protection didn't appear until 1972. In fact, the word *taboo* likely derives from "tapua," a Polynesian word for menstruation.

## spin doctoring

Starting in the 1930s, Tampax's packaging bore the slogan, "Accepted for Advertising by the American Medical Association." Tampax wasn't endorsed by the AMA—it simply had paid ads in the AMA Journal. The misleading slogan was nixed in 1943.

## unmarked vehicle

Buying feminine protection was so embarrassing in the 1920s that Kotex began selling its products in unmarked brown boxes. The marketing scheme didn't last long since competitors began using the same packaging.

## mommy dearest

A survey of American ninth-graders found that most girls think their mothers should broach the subject of menstruation with them first and provide emotional support. Sixty-nine percent of the girls also had succinct advice for their fathers: "Don't interfere."

## demo sale

In the 1930s, the first Tampax salesman peddled his wares to druggists by feigning thirst and asking for a drink of water. He then plopped a tampon into the water to demonstrate absorbency.

# hair color

The mastermind behind the twentieth century revolution in home hair coloring was not a chemist, a cosmetologist, or a coiffeur, but a New York copywriter named Shirley Polykoff. The slogans she penned for Clairol in the 1950s almost single-handedly squashed the social taboo against hair coloring in America and launched what is today a billion-dollar industry.

The seeds of Polykoff's advertising genius go back to the 1930s. One night, after a meet-the-parents dinner, Polykoff asked her boyfriend if his mother liked her. After a few evasive comments, he answered, "My mother says you paint your hair...Well, do you?" Polykoff did, and she did at a time when colored hair was seen as an emblem of actresses and prostitutes. Accepted opinion was that "nice" women didn't dye their hair. Those with the nerve to challenge convention colored hair secretly at home or in private salon rooms. Social censure was so harsh that some women only went to salons under an alias.

In 1956, Polykoff was working as a junior copywriter when she was asked to pen a slogan for Miss Clairol, the first home hair dye that colored, shampooed, and conditioned all in one step. Playing on the humiliating question she was asked years before about her hair, Polykoff came up with the lines "Does she or doesn't she? Hair color so natural only her hairdresser knows for sure!" Although the ad campaign featured attractive but unglamorous women posing with children—a not-so-subtle hint that hair color was respectable enough for wives and mothers—magazine editors thought the slogan was too suggestive. They refused to print the ads at first, but eventually relented. The ads went on to run for eighteen years, during which time Clairol sales more than quadrupled. The number of women coloring their hair soared from a measly 7 percent in the 1950s to more than 50 percent by the 1990s.

## feminine persuasion

More and more men are using hair color, but surveys show that nearly half of all men dyeing their hair for the first time are coaxed into taking the plunge by a woman.

## origin of the species

Modern synthetic hair color was created in 1907 by a French chemist named Éugene Schueller. He dubbed his creation Aureole, which means "halo" or "circle of light." A few years later, he started a fledgling company and called it L'Oréal.

## wretched recipes

An Egyptian hair color dating from 1200 B.C. consisted of dried tadpoles crushed in oil. A Roman formula called for a crow's egg and putrefied leeches mixed with black wine.

## air rage

In the early 1960s, airlines would not allow flight attendants to dye their hair. One executive railed, "If you let those girls run wild, there's no telling what could happen. They might end up with green hair to match the seat coverings."

## splitting hairs

According to surveys, men who dye their hair are more likely to use online services, drive sports cars, listen to jazz, and read books. Men who don't dye their hair are more likely to attend tractor pulls, drive a station wagon, go hunting, and collect stamps.

## venus and mars

"Does she or doesn't she?" was the slogan Clairol used to suggest their hair-dye colors were indistinguishable from natural ones. Polls showed that women did not think the slogan was sexually suggestive. Predictably, men did.

GENTLE NO-AMMONIA COLORANT

**20** WALNUT *Medium Ash Brown* 39 ml 1.35 FL.OZ.

# hair dryers

If inventions are born, then the hair dryer arrived as a set of twins. The two earliest hand-held electric models were produced by two different companies, but through an act of either cosmic convergence or corporate espionage they wound up debuting in the very same city in the very same year: Racine, Wisconsin, in 1920. The Race was made by the Racine Universal Motor Company while the equally speedy-sounding Cyclone was made by Hamilton Beach. These early dryers had casings of stainless steel or aluminum and employed fractional horsepower motors—small electric motors borrowed from other home appliances such as sewing machines and blenders. Until plastic casings were introduced in the 1930s, hair dryers remained heavy, clunky, and scorching hot to the touch.

The idea for the hair dryer, strangely, spun off from the vacuum cleaner. In the 1910s, home appliances were often marketed as multifunctional. One early vacuum cleaner ad showed a woman drying her hair with a stream of warm air spewing from the vacuum's exhaust. While recycling perfectly good air was a noble idea, it's unlikely that vacuums were seen as indispensible beauty aids. Nevertheless, the concept of blow drying was now established.

The sophistication of hair dryers increased in the 1930s and 1940s as variable speed and temperature settings were added. Today's hair dryers are so high-tech that some models even have two handles to optimize blow drying angles; others use infrared sensing technology to detect hair temperature and adjust heat levels automatically.

Hair dryer enthusiasts received a shock when consumer advocates discovered in 1979 that many heat shields and liners in hair dryers were made of asbestos—a known cancer-causing agent. Thankfully, the offending models were pulled from store shelves, and the only danger of using a hair dryer today is holding it too close and frying your 'do.

## doing the ironing

The curling iron, a cousin of the hair dryer, was first used by the Assyrians thirty-five hundred years ago. Both women and men of the noble classes curled their locks with heated iron bars.

## hotbed of activity

There must have been something in the drinking water: Racine, Wisconsin, is not only the birthplace of the hair dryer, but also the home of first electric milk shake mixer and the blender.

## blowing the case

In the late 1990s, the demand for salon blow-outs—hair straightening done with a hair dryer—increased dramatically. The most famous one might belong to Marcia Clark, the prosecuting attorney who debuted her blow-out during the O.J. Simpson trial.

## risky business

In parts of southern India, some women believe that hair drying is an activity fraught with potential danger. This is because Gangamma, the Goddess of Disguises, was once attacked by a lustful human as she dried her hair after a bath.

## total meltdown

In 1999, a full-sized, intact mammoth, complete with internal organs, was found frozen in the Siberian tundra. Scientists defrosted the beast's woolly hair inch by inch using hair dryers.

## overhead compartment

In 1951, Sears & Roebuck's fall/winter catalog featured the Ann Barton—the first helmeted hair dryer for home use. The dryer blew hot air into a pink plastic bonnet that sat on a woman's head.

HOT
WARM
COOL

HIGH
LOW
OFF

# hair removers

The appearance of hair on women's bodies has been judged through the ages as both sexy and repulsive. Depending on the whims of fashion, women either have proudly borne the shaggy look or endlessly shaved, waxed, and plucked in the name of beauty. Archeological evidence suggests that the self-torture began in India thousands of years ago when women started removing hair with abrasive pastes and resinous plasters. In ancient Egypt, people began eschewing hairy bodies after discovering unshaven armpits were smellier.

The first literary reference to underarm hair removal was made in the first century b.c. by Ovid in *The Art of Love-Making*. He eloquently penned: "I warn you that no rude goat find its way beneath your arms." Roman women took the warning to heart and applied an ancient depilatory to their underarms. Sadly, the active ingredient in the hair-melting paste was arsenic, which not only removed hair off women's bodies but also years off their lives.

The modern fashion for hairless bodies has uncertain origins. Photos of nudes taken before 1915, including Muybridge's studies of the human body in motion, show American women did not shave their armpits. Ribald French postcards of the era suggest women across the Atlantic also went *au naturel*. But after 1915, women began plucking underarm hair again. The reason for the revival is debatable, but many point to the influence of Hollywood. In the "Bathing Beauty" films of director Mack Sennett, for example, women sported sleeveless tops and shaved armpits. This look was adopted by flappers during the 1920s, and denuded underarms have been a standard of female beauty ever since. As hemlines rose above the ankles during the twentieth century, women also began shaving legs. American women, who wield their razors over ten times a month, have the cleanest-shaven legs in the world today. European women, however, don't seem to mind a few bristles—they only shave half as often.

## bad pluck

During the Middle Ages, excessive vanity was seen as a sin. Some medieval paintings even warned of the suffering in hell by depicting Satan plucking hairs out of vain babies with red hot tweezers.

### hair-razing demands

In the tenth century B.C., King Solomon reputedly agreed to make love to the Queen of Sheba on one condition: that she first remove "nature's veil."

### humorous

During the Italian Renaissance, body hair was in style. It was only removed when doctors shaved hysterical women in order to help the "suffocating humors of the brain" flow out more quickly.

### we wear short shorts

Of the women who remove leg hair, about half prefer shaving, a quarter prefer waxing, while the rest prefer electric appliances and hair-melting creams. Contary to popular belief, shaving does not make hair grow back darker, thicker, or faster.

### bug off

The exact origin of underarm shaving in the U.S. is unclear, but some believe prostitutes in California during the gold rush were the first to take up the practice. They shaved their underarms to prove they had no body lice—a big problem in the Wild West.

### razor envy

Despite the fact that women's razors are angled differently to prevent nicks and allow women to see more of the skin on their legs while shaving, studies show that women largely prefer razors made for men.

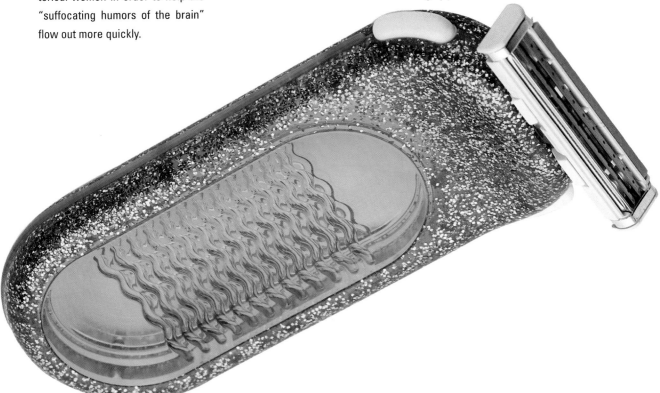

# hairpins

When early humans wanted to prevent their tresses from flying into a tousled mess ten thousand years ago, they reached for the nearest slender bone or thorn to skewer their hair. In time, people learned to fashion their own hairpins out of wood, ivory, bronze, silver, or gold. The first hairpins were long and straight. Many were plain, but others were sumptuously decorated, often having an ornamental crown. The women of ancient Greece often twisted their hair into a knot on the top of their heads where it was fastened using a pin adorned with a cicada or flower. Roman women also wore fanciful pins, and one type even had a hollow designed to hold poison—the type Cleopatra supposedly used to poison herself.

In the Far East, hair ornaments were the most important form of jewelry until the 1800s. Japanese women wore their hair in specific traditional styles that signaled age, class, marital status, or occupation, and a plethora of pins were needed to keep the hairdos in place. In China, hairpins were often adorned with inlays of iridescent blue feathers from the tiny kingfisher bird. The feathers were so prized that they were sent by Chinese farmers to the Imperial Court in Beijing as tributes. Mass production ruined the quality of kingfisher hairpins by the 1880s, and the last Chinese factory to make the jewelry closed in 1930.

The first hairpins made of bent wire were produced in England, and were being exported to France by 1545. These small U-shaped pins were an instant hit and soon made straight pins virtually obsolete. Bronze and iron were the first materials used, but tempered steel became standard by the nineteenth century. Originally, both tines of a hairpin were straight, but zigzag crimping was later added to one tine to help keep hairpins in place. In addition to the classic black lacquered hairpin, there is now a full arsenal of clasps, clips, sticks, and barrettes available to the modern woman to help keep her hair just so.

## picky picky

Some traditional Japanese hairpins had small earpicks on one end that looked like tiny spoons. The picks were also used to scratch the scalp once elaborate hairdos were set.

## etymologically speaking

The seventeenth century wig craze in Europe required a person's real hair to be cut into a short "bob," and the small U-shaped pins that were used to hold hair down soon became known as "bobby pins."

## motion detectors

Up until the nineteenth century, Chinese mandarins wore hairpins that featured small metallic decorations mounted on springs. When wearers moved their heads even slightly, the decorations would elegantly bob and sway.

## unfair advantage

Japanese geishas are trained traditional entertainers and not highly paid prostitutes, but they do sometimes play stripping games to amuse clients. A geisha never loses since she is still pulling out her many hairpins by the time a man has lost his shirt and tie.

## cost of production

The first hairpins produced in the U.S. were likely made of horn. The material was first softened by being boiled in whale oil for several days, a process which filled the homes of comb makers with a nauseating stench.

## patrician preference

Queen Shubad of Mesopotamia (circa 3000 B.C.) wore long gold hairpins. Cleopatra (69–30 B.C.), on the other hand, favored ivory hairpins studded with jewels.

# hairstyling products

Hairstyling products are marvels of modern science. Gels and hairsprays contain synthetic polymers that lock hair in place. Mousses make use of humectants, moisture-absorbing chemicals that expand hairs to boost natural curl and body, while volumizers coat hair strands with resins to give coifs more thickness and bounce. Modern styling products, which have existed for less than a century, make doing up a 'do far more pleasant than in the past. Today's fashion junkies no longer have to sculpt their locks with pungent oils, sticky grease, beef marrow gels, fatty soap, or animal dung as our ancestors once did.

The first aerosol hairspray was launched in the United States in 1949, and women's hairstyles soon began reaching skyward. The earliest fixative in hairspray was shellac, normally used to varnish wood. It provided high luster and good hold, but was insoluble in water and exhausting to wash out. Undeterred, women ditched their bobs and ponytails for buns and beehives. Not to be left out, men also smothered their hair with generous gobs of products. Chief among them was Brylcreem. Sales of Brylcreem peaked at more than $25 million a year in the 1950s as young men took to aping the well-greased locks of Elvis or James Dean. But with the coming of the Beatles and their mop-top haircuts in the early 1960s, hairstyles relaxed and sales of Brylcreem and other styling products crashed.

"Big hair" made a big comeback in the 1980s. People began rediscovering the gravity-defying wonders of gel, first introduced in the mid-1960s, as well as hairspray, which was now water-soluble. Add to these staples a full range of other products such as mousses, texturizers, and root-lifters, and there was no hair that couldn't be poufed, feathered, spiked, or teased. In the 1990s, messy, unkempt hair became a hot fashion look for men, but don't be fooled by the seemingly low-maintenance coif. Men can now buy special "bed head" products to help them achieve a fashionably tousled top.

## big bash

The logo of L'Oréal's Studio Line brand of products pays homage to the Dutch modernist group de Stijl (the Style). Formed during World War I, the group worked with geometric forms and primary colors, and was dedicated to the "absolute devaluation of tradition."

## fancy free

Studies show that consumers show little or no brand loyalty towards hairstyling products. Men are particularly nonchalant—they tend to use poorer quality products than women.

## oil slick

In the late 1800s, a greasy Indonesian oil known as macassar became a sought-after hairstyling product for men. This lead to the creation of antimacassars, crocheted doilies draped over chair backs and sofas to absorb excess oil and protect upholstery.

## straight to the top

Sarah Walker Breedlove became the first female African-American millionaire after creating a line of hair pomades and hot combs for straightening hair. Before Walker's products hit the market, women straightened tightly curled hair on ironing boards.

## the mane idea

Women start styling hair from an early age. According to toy makers, the most common play pattern exhibited by girls with fashion dolls such as Barbie is "hair play."

## taking the pitch

English cricketer and footballer Denis Compton became the first "Brylcreem Boy" in the 1940s. In 1997, English football star David Beckham was signed for the same role. Compton earned ten thousand pounds for his endorsement—Beckham received one million.

# laxatives

An American doctor named W. H. Graves felt that the most vital health question of the twentieth century was, "How well do we eliminate?" The answer: not very well. After humans settled into an agrarian way of life thousands of years ago, diets steadily became higher in fat and lower in roughage. Rich foods clogged our bowels, and the good doctor Graves even surmised that 90 percent of all illnesses were the result of constipation. He was wrong, of course, but today's greasy diets do leave millions of people desperate for a potent laxative.

The most celebrated purgative of all time is Ex-Lax. It was introduced in 1906 by a Hungarian immigrant to the United States, Max Kiss. The active ingredient in Ex-Lax was phenolphthalein, a chemical popularly known as an acid-base indicator. It was used by winemakers to gauge the acidity of their goods, but what was thought to be an innocuous additive soon proved to have messy side effects. Kiss tried a small dose on himself to confirm the purgative effects. Then genius struck: he hit upon the idea of combining phenolphthalein with chocolate to make a laxative that even children would find palatable. Kiss initially christened his laxative Bo-Bo (for bon-bon, to stress its sweet taste), but later renamed it Ex-Lax—short for "excellent laxative." Behind the slogan "When Nature forgets, remember Ex-Lax," sales eventually soared to more than five hundred million doses a year.

Humans have used laxatives for at least thirty-five hundred years. Popular ancient purgatives included castor oil, aloe vera, linseed, and rhubarb. When studies suggested in the 1990s that phenolphthalein posed potential health risks, the makers of Ex-Lax turned to the past for a safer replacement. They found it in senna, a tropical shrub containing a powerful laxative in its leaves. Senna was widely used centuries ago in Europe, Asia, Africa, and pre-Columbian America, proving that "staying regular" is not just a modern health fad, but an age-old obsession.

## taste of one's own medicine

In the early 1900s, the makers of Ex-Lax introduced a fig-flavored version of their laxative. It sold poorly compared to chocolate Ex-Lax and was quickly discontinued.

## safe passage

Laxative chemicals in seed-bearing fruit can cause some birds to excrete ingested seeds sooner. This provides a biological advantage to the fruit species. Seeds that pass through birds faster are less digested and show higher rates of germination.

## unobstructed view

Dr. John H. Kellogg, the inventor of Corn Flakes, wrote the book *Colon Hygiene* in 1917. In it he opined: "The prompt evacuation of the bowels in response to Nature's 'call' is a sacred obligation which no person can neglect without serious injury."

## take the money and run it

Laxative advertisements began to appear more frequently on the radio during the Great Depression because radio stations couldn't afford to turn away sponsors.

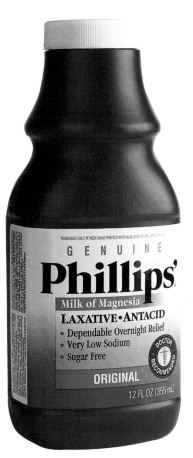

## every trick in the book

An ancient Egyptian recipe for relieving constipation called for an old book to be boiled in oil. Egyptians didn't think books had special curative properties—old books were simply an economical source of plant fibers.

## winnie the pooh

Maybe this is why Winnie ate so much honey: it has a laxative effect. Honey contains high amounts of fructose, a sugar that some people cannot digest properly, and this can lead to a hyper-active bowel.

# linoleum

In most people's minds, linoleum is synonymous with "tacky." But the drab bathroom flooring many of us call linoleum is more often than not actually made of vinyl, a synthetic petroleum-based material. True linoleum, which earned a bad reputation and went out of fashion in the 1950s, is an all-natural flooring that has many good qualities.

Linoleum is a direct descendant of oil cloths. In the 1700s, Europeans looking for a waterproof flooring brushed coats of linseed oil over swaths of stretched canvas. Once the oil stiffened, the smooth surface that resulted was easy to clean—and easy to paint. Oil cloths mimicking Roman mosaics or Turkish carpets became a "must" in households with more taste than money. Laid over floorings such as wood, oil cloths saved more precious surfaces from wear and tear. However, the limited lifespan of canvas spurred the search for an even more resilient flooring.

The answer was found in 1860 when Frederick Walton, an English oil cloth maker, combined linseed oil, ground cork, sawdust, pine resins, and limestone with a strong burlap backing. This produced a material that was flexible, durable, and inexpensive. Because linseed oil (*linum oleum* in Latin) was its key ingredient, the new material was termed "linoleum." Some early users simply laid down sheets of linoleum like an area rug, but Walton's brainchild found its true calling as wall-to-wall flooring. Linoleum proved to have many benefits. As linseed oil oxidizes with age, it not only becomes harder and more durable, but it also gives off a gas that retards the growth of bacteria. This made linoleum the obvious flooring choice for many hospitals. Linoleum is also anti-static (which keeps dust and dust mites at bay), as well as nonflammable. Most importantly, though, linoleum's all-natural ingredients readily biodegrade when dumped in a landfill. Many people are now rediscovering these virtues and realizing linoleum isn't so tacky after all.

## foreign affairs

To make the world's first piece of linoleum in 1860, Englishman Frederick Walton used Siberian flaxseed, Spanish cork, New Zealand pine resin, and Indian jute fibers.

### one hit wonder

In the 1850s, Englishman Elijah Galloway made a linoleum-like flooring by combining powdered cork and molten rubber. He named it "kamptulicon." Though installed in the less important parts of the Houses of Parliament, it soon faded into obscurity.

### endangered species

Linoleum fell out of favor in the 1950s since vinyl sheeting was easier to produce. To add insult to injury, even the word "linoleum" is going out of style. Linoleum is now often referred to as "Marmoleum," which is actually a brand name.

### a cut above

Linocuts are relief prints made by cutting into soft linoleum. Since linoleum is easier to cut than wood, linocut was despised by many artists as technically undemanding until art-world giants Picasso and Matisse used and legitimized the technique.

### all decked out

When the U.S. Navy needed a tough, non-skid, and non-reflective deck surface for their ships in the late 1800s, it turned to linoleum. Today, the heaviest grades of plain linoleum are still called "battleship" linoleum.

### takes a kicking, keeps on ticking

New York's Radio City Music Hall offers proof of linoleum's durability. The high-heeled Rockettes have kicked their way to fame across the same linoleum floor for more than twenty-five years.

# lip balm

Only one in three people suffer from chapped lips, yet an estimated 60 percent of adults use lip balm. Even for those with healthy lips, smearing a layer of waxy goo around the mouth can become something of a security blanket. Some people apply lip balm dozens of times a day and suffer mild panic attacks when deprived of their favorite lip relief. Chapping, however, is really not a medical calamity. It occurs because the outer layer of lip skin is like a sponge: it can absorb moisture quickly, but when it dries out, it becomes hard and prone to cracking. Left untreated, chapped lips will eventually heal themselves, but most people prefer not to leave lip-conditioning up to their body's natural defenses.

The seeds of the lip balm craze were first sown by Dr. C. D. Fleet of Virginia. In the early 1880s, he combined petroleum and wax into a molded stick that looked like a wickless candle. Fleet wrapped the product in foil and sold it locally as a dry lip remedy. He named it Chap Stick. After peddling his creation for years without much success, Fleet sold the rights to another Virginia resident named John Morton for a mere five dollars.

Morton and his wife churned out Chap Stick from their own home. Mrs. Morton melted the pinkish mixture on her kitchen stove, poured it into brass tubes, and set the tubes on the porch to cool. Morton then pushed out the waxy sticks, cut and wrapped them, and shipped the balm to druggists across the country. Chap Stick got its big break when the U.S. government bought large quantities to issue to its troops during World War II—in olive-drab tubes, no less. Servicemen returning home after the war continued to buy the product and sales soared. Of course, Chap Stick production is no longer a homemade affair. Today, Chap Stick's production line pumps out eighty-five thousand units during a regular shift. And with dozens of other brands on the market, lip balm junkies need not fear—there's no shortage of supply.

## sealed with a kiss

Lips have something in common with fingerprints: no two lip impressions are exactly alike.

### thin-skinned

Lip skin is the most vulnerable on the body. Even the reddest of lips lack melanin, the pigment that blocks UV rays. Lip skin also loses moisture quickly because it has only one to three epidermal layers, whereas the rest of our skin has eight to fifteen.

### "we love you, kevin"

In 1995, San Francisco librarian Kevin C. founded Lip Balm Anonymous, a support group that offers a twelve-step program for kicking the lip balm habit. Despite urban myths, there is no scientific evidence that proves lip balm is chemically addictive.

### casualty of war

Carmex lip balm was created in 1937, but remained a homemade product until after World War II. During the war, Carmex production slowed because a key ingredient, lanolin, was used by the U.S. military to grease war equipment.

### most wanted list

Blistex lip balm was launched in 1947. Since 1980, the brand has published an annual list of the world's most beautiful and desirable lips. Past winners include Michael Jordan, Cameron Diaz, and Arnold Schwarzenegger.

### udder-ly soothing

Many Americans looking for lip relief swear by Bag Balm, a dry-skin ointment made for animals since 1899. It is normally applied to areas such as cow udders.

# lipstick

The rise of modern lipstick helped topple nineteenth century taboos against the use of cosmetics in the West. With the Americans and the British preaching prudery and the French sending lipstick-wearers to the guillotine, makeup use declined sharply in the early 1800s. Cosmetics were seen as insincere and uncouth, fit for only prostitutes and actors. Not surprisingly, the first lip coloring in stick form was designed by German Charles Meyer in the 1860s for use in the theater.

Lipstick finally escaped its life of exile in the playhouses when the French company Guerlain introduced a grapefruit lipstick in 1880. This was perhaps the first appearance of lipstick on store shelves, and it was an immediate success. American Maurice Levy added fuel to the comeback when he packaged lipstick in a sliding metal tube in 1915. The biggest boost for lipstick, however, was the emergence of the new art of film. The silver screen set the fashion trends for the masses, and no craze was hotter than lipstick. By the 1920s, cosmetics—spurred by massive lipstick sales—was the fourth largest industry in America behind only cars, movies, and bootlegged liquor.

Before the days of the sliding tube, lipcolor came as a powder or paste. The first known lipcolor, found in a Sumerian tomb, dates back five thousand years. In the first century b.c., Cleopatra used a powder of henna and crushed red insects. Greek women favored paints made of mulberry or seaweed. Stylish ladies of the Indus Valley used lac-dye, while those of the Far East dabbed their lower lips with gold. For most of history, lipstick production was a homemade affair. Sadly, many hack chemists died at the hands of their own toxic creations. The woman of today has no such worry—she simply goes shopping, buying an average of four tubes a year. Over a lifetime, a typical woman consumes up to nine pounds of lipstick, proving that lipstick is back with a vengeance and definitely here to stay.

## licking their chops
Women wind up ingesting about 50 percent of their lipstick.

## lipstick service

During World War II, the U.S. government conducted tests and determined that wearing lipstick boosted women's morale. Orders were then given to stock factory dressing rooms with lipstick to improve worker efficiency.

## kiss and makeup

Queen Victoria publicly declared in the nineteenth century that makeup was impolite. Victorian women who wanted to add a dash of color to their lips resorted to kissing rosy crepe paper on the sly.

## my lips aren't sealed

Max Factor, an early pioneer of modern lipstick, spouted in 1958, "A woman who doesn't wear lipstick feels undressed in public. Unless she works on a farm."

## fishing for compliments

Lipstick that glitters contains particles which reflect and scatter light. Additives that do the trick include tiny specks of silica, mica, or ground fish scales.

## the gap

The idea of a "generation gap" between parents and children is commonplace today, but this wasn't always so. One of the first references to the concept was in 1925 when people began noting the growing chasm between daughters who wore lipstick and mothers who did not.

# mirrors

In today's world of space flight and computer gadgetry, mirrors seem decidedly low-tech. Yet, mirror production once represented the cutting edge of human technological achievement. Mirror manufacturing generated huge economic benefits—a fact that inspired rival nations to go to extraordinary lengths to safeguard or steal mirror-making secrets.

The modern glass mirror emerged from the furnaces of Venice in the fourteenth century. Artisans backed greenish plates of glass with metallic leaf, creating a reflecting surface that was superior to the polished metal mirrors of antiquity. Eager to guard their know-how, the Venetian glassblowers' guild moved the entire glass and mirror industry to a local island. Workers caught leaving the island or smuggling out scrap glass were punished by death. In 1460, the Venetians invented transparent glass, and in 1507, they began backing clear glass with an amalgam of mercury and tin. This new mirror was in such high demand throughout Europe that Venice's mirror makers enjoyed a lucrative monopoly for well over a century.

The monopoly was shattered in 1664 when French authorities under Louis XIV bribed and smuggled a group of mirror makers out of Italy. Red-faced Venetian officials offered safe-passage, pardons, and money to artisans willing to return. The French quickly countered by bringing the wives of several artisans to Paris, and persuading Louis XIV to greet the mirror makers personally. This was the last straw for Venetian officials. They resolved to murder the defectors, and before long, two mirror makers were found poisoned to death. Frightened, many of the Venetian émigrés returned home, but the damage was done: knowledge of mirror making was leaked and new rivals to the Venetian cartel slowly emerged. By the time the modern process of silvering glass was discovered in 1835, mirrors were no longer seen as high-tech luxuries, but as prosaic necessities of daily life.

## seeing is relieving

The ancient Chinese believed that mirrors could ward off evil specters since spirits did not want to "be seen" by a mirror.

## grave discoveries

The world's oldest mirrors, found in Turkish gravesites, are made of polished volcanic glass and date back to 6000 B.C. The earliest known metal mirror, found in an Egyptian tomb, is made of bronze and dates from 2900 B.C.

## alarming

The Aztecs created an early home security system by leaving a knife in a bowl of water by the door. Would-be thieves, seeing their reflection pierced by the knife, quickly turned and ran in fear.

## payment plan

The superstition that a broken mirror leads to seven years' bad luck may be related to the notion that mirrors hold the soul. Or it may simply stem from the fact that early glass mirrors were so outrageously expensive that an average person who broke a mirror might have had to save for seven years to buy a replacement.

## life insurance

From Europe to Madagascar, some people still cover mirrors or turn them to the wall after a death in the house. They believe that their soul, reflected in the mirror, can be carried away by the ghost of the deceased.

## mirror, mirror off-the-wall

In sixteenth century Europe, carrying hand or pocket mirrors was wildly popular among the well-to-do. Moralists of the time, however, condemned acts of self-admiration or self-grooming in a mirror as decadent and sinful. This criticism soon sparked another fashion craze: carrying pocket mirrors disguised as prayer books.

# moisturizer

Very Dry Skin
Peau très sèche

Ninety-five percent of uncomplicated skin problems are related to dehydration. Today, we can seek out skin care advice from lab coat-clad beauticians, but seven thousand years ago, our ancestors had to figure out for themselves how to guard against the ravages of dry skin. Nomads in the Nile Valley learned to smear their bodies with castor oil—perhaps the world's first moisturizer. By the time the Egyptians settled into an agricultural way of life around 3500 B.C., protecting the skin from the searing sun had become a national obsession. Ointments typically were made of nine parts animal fat and one part perfumed resin, and were often used in special "unguent" rooms built for cleaning and anointing the body. Ironically, many of these skin creams were first developed for preserving mummies.

Some early lotions were of suspect value. An Egyptian recipe combined gazelle dung, hippopotamus fat, and writing fluid, while others called for animal genitalia—an ingredient widely believed in the ancient world to restore youth and beauty. But one early concoction has endured through the centuries: cold cream. It was first made in the second century a.d. by the Greek physician Galen. His recipe called for rose buds to be steeped in a mixture of melted white wax, olive oil, and water. The term "cold cream" comes from the fact that in the early 1900s, druggists often kept the product fresh by storing it on ice.

## too many ups and down

Some flight attendants complain of premature wrinkling, but dry cabin air is not to blame. Instead, it's the pull of gravity stretching the skin every time a plane takes off or lands that worsens wrinkling.

For centuries, the only way people moisturized was with fatty, greasy-feeling creams, but a skin care revolution came in 1912 when a German chemist created Nivea—the world's first "non-greasy" moisturizer. Nivea was the first stable water-in-oil emulsion and it nourished the skin without feeling "heavy." Men used it as an after-shave lotion, women as an all-purpose salve. Nivea revolutionized the beauty industry. Fat-based creams became a thing of the past, and today no one has to put up with greasy goop on their skin to keep it soft and supple.

## variations on a theme

The world's bestselling facial moisturizer is known as Oil of Olay in North America, Oil of Ulay in England, Oil of Olaz in continental Europe, and Oil of Ulan in Asia and Africa. The various names are meant to sound more pleasing to different cultures.

## opportunity knocks

American Dr. George Bunting created a sunburn lotion in 1914. After a customer tried the cream on his itchy skin, he raved, "Doc, your cream sure knocked my eczema." This inspired Bunting to rename his product Noxzema.

## laudable ideas

Clinique salespeople were the first to wear white lab coats. Clinique is owned by Estée Lauder, the beauty guru who pioneered another industry staple: free cosmetics samples.

## big bird balm

For centuries, native Australians have moisturized their skin with emu fat. It is so effective that doctors have begun using it to soothe skin after chemical peels and laser resurfacing.

## alpha females

Cleopatra bathed in spoiled milk, while ladies of the French court washed with spoiled wine. Both liquids contained alpha-hydroxy acids—popular and effective ingredients found in modern day skin care products.

# mouthwash

To put it plainly, there is no social sin deadlier than having bad breath. Novelist George Orwell once opined, "You can have affection for a murderer, but you cannot have affection for a man whose breath smells." Orwell was hardly exaggerating. The mere thought that others might catch a whiff of our breath and proclaim it a disaster drives us to spend billions yearly on mints, gum, and mouthwashes to pre-empt potential humiliation.

One of the first records of mouthwash was made in a Chinese text dating back five thousand years. It suggested the mouth be rinsed with urine. This was not just a bit of ancient Chinese foolishness—many other cultures also did the same. The Romans used urine for mouthwashes and toothpaste, while the early Germans advised that the first urine of the day was the best for gargling purposes. Urine from a healthy person is sterile and contains ammonia, the cleansing agent that our distant ancestors were unwittingly making use of.

The age of modern mouthwashes began with the launch of Listerine in 1880. It was created as a general antiseptic by American Dr. Joshua Lawrence and named after Sir Joseph Lister, a pioneer of sterile surgery. Although Listerine enjoyed steady sales as a cure for everything from dandruff to athlete's foot, it did not become a household name until it was promoted as a bad breath remedy in the 1920s. Company executives seized upon the suitably awful-sounding word "halitosis"—it was used often in early ads—and promised that the condition could be banished with a good swish of Listerine. In the 1940s and '50s, Listerine pulled no punches in painting those with bad breath as social pariahs. One ad told of "Edna," who was "Often a bridesmaid, but never a bride." In another, a man rings a doorbell while his friends inside shriek, "Here comes Herb! For Pete's sake, duck!" The ads helped make Listerine the market-leader in mouthwashes, and bad breath the social blunder of the century.

## flower power

The ancient Romans of all classes used perfume to conceal body odors. Some even drank perfume straight or mixed it with wine to hide bad breath.

### secret service

In 1968, Proctor and Gamble asked people to secretly send in the names and addresses of their smelly breathed friends. Proctor and Gamble then mailed rebate coupons for Scope mouthwash to the oral offenders.

### the morning after

Humans are blessed with a natural mouthwash that carries away bacteria: saliva. Sadly, saliva production slows during sleep, drying our mouths and leaving us with the infamous funk known as morning breath.

### kissed off

When Scope revealed survey results in 1997 proclaiming American talk show host Rosie O'Donnell one of the least kissable celebrities, Listerine helped her fight back by donating $1,000 each time Rosie was kissed by a guest on her show. The promotion raised thousands for charity and bad press for Scope.

### unholy taste

Myrrh, a gummy tree resin once given to the baby Jesus by the three wise men, has been used in mouthwashes since Biblical times. Many who have tried myrrh mouthwashes say its tastes awful.

### past lives

Listerine's 25 percent alcohol content made the mouthwash a popular beverage during Prohibition in America. In the 1940s, Listerine was even marketed as a hair tonic.

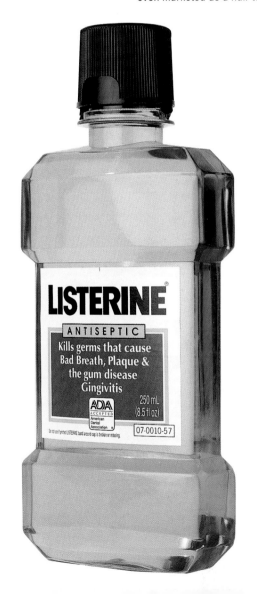

# nail polish

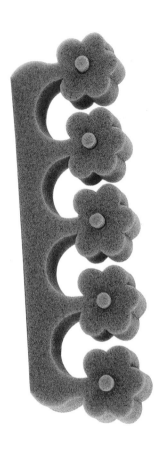

When modern liquid nail polishes were launched in 1907, they were such a novelty that *Vogue* had to explain to its readers how to use the clear polishes step-by-step. Before this time, women who grew up in the cosmetics-starved nineteenth century did little more than buff their nails with powder or a chamois. But after throwing off the chains of socially prescribed modesty, women took to nail polishes with a passion.

Cutex launched the first tinted nail polish in 1917, made from natural resins colored with dyes. True nail enamel, however, didn't appear for another decade. It had a pinkish color, and was only applied to the middle of the nail, leaving the white tips and half moon bare. Red and other bold colors became chic by 1930. That same year, fashion magazines first reported that nail colors were being coordinated with lipstick. By the 1950s, 90 percent of teenage girls were wearing nail polish, and 18 percent had started before they were ten.

Nail polish later became a victim of its own success. The long nails and showy colors favored by status-conscious women in the excessive 1980s lead to a cultural backlash in the early 1990s when shorter, uncolored nails were considered "classier." French nails and other simple styles made a big comeback. Nail polish mania, however, was resuscitated when Chanel created a red polish for their catwalk models in March of 1994. Fashion hounds clamored to get their hands on the product, and in August it was launched to the American public as Vamp. By the time it reached the United Kingdom as Rouge Noir in 1995, it had already achieved cult status by appearing on Uma Thurman's nails in *Pulp Fiction*. Vamp would go on to become Chanel's best-selling product ever.

Today, gender equity pervades the cosmetics world and more men are painting their nails, but they don't have to give up their "manliness" to do it. Nail colors for men include Uzi, Asphalt, Gigolo, Superman, and of course, Testosterone.

## as advertised

In 1966, Estée Lauder prepared forty-one shades of nail polish for the summer season, one of which was called 24K Gold. The product actually contained pure gold.

## primeval polish

The ancient Egyptians stained their fingernails with orange henna, but the practice of painting nails as we know it today originated in China five thousand years ago. Nail lacquers were made of Arabic gum, vegetable dyes, egg white, beeswax, and gelatin.

## job retraining

During World War I, Chaim Weizmann invented a method of synthesizing acetone for the British explosives industry. Acetone later became known as nail polish remover, and Weizmann went on to become the first president of modern Israel in 1949.

## nailing it down

Doctors can use the growth pattern of fingernails to diagnose disease. Nails can show nutrient deficiencies and even give telltale signs of emphysema, bronchitis, liver disease, and heart-valve infections.

## be true to your school

In the late 1990s when the craze for men's nail polish began, some high school football coaches in the United States ordered bulk quantities of nail polish in school colors for players to wear on game day.

## ten times platinum

In 1931, nail colors were mostly pinkish, but arbiters of style in Paris began approving of bright nail colors, especially for evening. "Platinum tips," opaque silver polish applied to the tips of red enameled nails, soon became a fashion must.

# perfume

In many Indo-European languages, the word for perfume comes from the Latin *per fumum*, meaning "through smoke." This is because the earliest perfumes were in fact incense. Humans first manipulated smells by burning fragrant woods and resins in primitive shrines to mask the gruesome stench of animal sacrifices. In time, incense itself became an offering to the gods. By 3000 b.c., aromatics were valuables in their own right, not only used to please the heavens, but also to pamper the body. The ancient Egyptians perfumed themselves by taking baths scented with iris and jasmine, or by placing a cone of aromatic fat on their heads and allowing the grease to slowly melt down their bodies. During Roman times, perfume was widely used to mask body odor, and even to scent bathroom walls.

In the Dark Ages, malodor became all the rage in Europe, and the great centers of perfumery shifted to the Middle East and Asia. In the tenth century a.d., Avicenna, the Arab scholar, extracted rose attar (oil) by pioneering the process of distillation. The Arabs used rose attar to purify mosques, scent gloves, honor houseguests, and even flavor food.

Interest in fragrance returned to Europe after the First Crusade of the eleventh century. While the campaign failed to bring back any religious converts, it did bring back invaluable knowledge of perfumery. By studying Arab texts, Europeans slowly improved the process of distillation, and in 1370, the first modern perfume was created. The fragrance was the first to use both essential oils and distilled alcohol. Made by a hermit and named "Hungary Water" for the Queen of Hungary, it remained a bestseller for more than four hundred years.

In the twentieth century, the French and the Americans emerged as the global sultans of scent, and their perfume industries and markets remain the biggest today. In France, nine in ten women wear perfume, while in the U.S., consumers spend over $5 billion on fragrances every year.

## a thorn in their side

When perfumers first extracted rose attar in the tenth century A.D., producing one measly ounce of attar required two hundred pounds of rose petals.

## cyber smells

The rise of organic chemistry in the 1800s led to the production of synthetic perfume ingredients, which have become just as important as natural ingredients. Today, perfumery is so high-tech that computers can "remember" natural smells and reproduce them artificially.

## mod squad

In 1889, the House of Guerlain in France produced Jicky, one of the first fragrances to use synthetics. Revered in the perfume world as the first of *Les Grands Parfums*, Jicky caused a public sensation with its "ferociously modern" smell.

## the nose knows

The most talented perfume designers in the world are called "noses." They have more than two thousand scents committed to memory and can distinguish each ingredient in a mix of a hundred or more.

## getting to the heart of the matter

One of the most important aromatics in India is sandalwood. To harvest sandalwood, loggers cut down a tree, allow tropical termites to attack the nonodorous outer layers, and then collect the scented and insect-resistant heartwood.

## making no scents

The Chinese and Japanese historically have tended to scent the environment more than the body itself. Some suggest a physiological reason for this: compared to Europeans, Asians have very few apocrine glands—the glands responsible for body odor.

# powder and foundation

The most tragic misstep in the history of cosmetics was the use of ceruse, a white facial powder applied to achieve the ghostly pallor that was fashionable in the West for thousands of years. From its debut in ancient Egyptian times until the nineteenth century, ceruse was generously dusted over women's faces, necks, and bosoms. The high levels of lead in ceruse, however, eventually ruined complexions and cut short lives. Rouge was just as deadly. It was often colored red with cinnabar, a poisonous form of mercury, which likely contributed to countless miscarriages, congenital defects, and stillbirths. Many men also powdered their faces in the ancient world and likewise suffered for their vanity.

Despite the deadly consequences, the use of powder and rouge ran riot in the eighteenth century. French women in particular prized chalk-white faces and flaming red cheeks, and were accused by critics of looking like "skinned sheep." Wearing blush, however, was such a fashion must that Madame de Pompadour, the mistress of Louis XV, passed away peacefully only after receiving her last rites and then rouging her face. British moralists of the day were so alarmed by the increasing use of makeup that a law was passed in 1770 stating women who lured men into marriage with the use of makeup would be prosecuted as witches. To their credit, English women paid little attention to the draconian law.

## filler up

Many homemade powders were of higher quality than store-bought ones in the 1800s. Commercially made products often contained cheap fillers such as nuts and potatoes.

In the nineteenth century, safer powders made of pounded rice, starch, and talc debuted. Lead was replaced with harmless metals such as bismuth, but they had a distressing tendency to react with sulphur fumes from coal fires and gas pipes and turn faces a dirty grey. Foolproof powders didn't emerge until the early twentieth century when various countries passed laws to ensure all cosmetics were tested for safety and efficacy. Nowadays, facial powders and foundations continue to enjoy popularity, forming the second-best selling cosmetics category after lipstick.

## foundations of foundation

The thin base of color we call "foundation" was created in the 1930s. The first water-soluble, matte foundation was developed by Hollywood makeup artist Max Factor in 1938. It came in dry, round cakes and was referred to as Pan Cake Makeup.

## mixed blessing

Elizabeth Arden has developed a computer system to produce custom foundation that perfectly matches a person's skin. The foundation, whipped up at a cosmetics counter in about ten minutes, can be mixed into forty-five billion color combinations.

## cleaning up

Clean Make-Up Liquid Foundation was launched in 1961 as the first cosmetic under the Cover Girl label. The water-based foundation contains Noxzema skin care ingredients, and now sells at the rate of one every second.

## sole sisters

In the early 1900s, most women used puffs, chamois skins, and coated papers to powder their faces. Some women, however, preferred a more efficient applicator: rabbit's feet.

powder brush

## looks that kill

In the beauty industry, an olive shade of powder is known as Rachel. The shade was named after a French tragic actress who was famous for her natural facial color. Sadly, her unique skin tone resulted from tuberculosis, which killed her in 1858 at the age of thirty-seven.

# razors

Men have been in search of a clean shave for at least thirty thousand years. Ancient cave paintings suggest our hairy forebears shaved with shells, animal horns, shark's teeth, and honed flint. These early disposable blades were used for millennia, but were replaced after the advent of metalwork. As early as 3000 b.c., reusable copper razors became popular in both Egypt and India, and by 1500 b.c., Scandinavians were embossing bronze razors with ornate designs. Razor technology remained largely unchanged until the 1700s when the steel straightedge, or cut-throat razor, was introduced in Sheffield, England. Users were justifiably nervous since shaving with the aptly named cut-throat was often a hazardous affair. Nevertheless, the straightedge remained in widespread use until disposable blades made a comeback in 1903—the year the Gillette Company of Boston launched the safety razor.

In the late nineteenth century, salesman King Camp Gillette was encouraged by his boss, William Painter, to create a product that could be used once and discarded. Painter himself had invented a throwaway bottle cap and profited handsomely. While shaving one morning, Gillette was struck with an idea. Instead of constantly honing a straightedge, Gillette envisioned shaving with a thin sliver of steel clamped in a guarded holder that would prevent serious cuts. When the blade became dull, it would simply be thrown away. Experts warned Gillette that making steel thin enough, hard enough, and cheap enough for disposable blades would be impossible. Undaunted, he hired a young engineer named William Nickerson who quickly overcame the technical hurdles. In 1903, the safety razor hit the U.S. market. Sales slumped in the first year (fifty-one razors and 168 blades), but exploded in the second (ninety thousand razors and 123,000 blades), sparking a shaving revolution that soon made Gillette a household name and the straightedge a thing of the past.

## clear cut policy

In 1705, Peter the Great decreed that Russia would be a beard-free zone. Men who refused to shave off their beards risked being taxed one hundred rubles or being thrown into jail.

### the hairy truth

Men have anywhere from six thousand to thirty thousand facial hair fibers that grow up to six inches per year. To combat this growth, the clean-shaven man will spend around three thousand hours, or 125 days, of his life shaving.

### great minds think alike

Five hundred years ago, the Aztecs shaved with shards of the volcanic glass obsidian. Tribal peoples of central Africa did the same up to the beginning of the twentieth century.

### hands off

The ancient Greeks and Romans encouraged the custom of shaving in the fourth century B.C. as a defensive measure for soldiers. Clean-shaven men could not be grasped by their facial hair during hand-to-hand combat.

### one track mind

Fidel Castro, the president of Cuba, told a television reporter in 1985 that he gave up shaving in order to free up ten days worth of time every year. He argued this time was better spent on revolutionary causes.

### shaving off time

According to the Guinness Book of World Records, the fastest barber ever is Denny Rowe of England. In 1988, he shaved 1,994 men in an hour using a straight razor—an impressive rate of one shave every 1.8 seconds. Only four unlucky men were nicked.

# running and hot water

For Europeans and Americans living in the 1800s, taking a bath was no easy feat. Country folks got their water from wells and pumps, and soon found that even over short distances the fatigue of lugging water far outweighed the pleasure of bathing. In poor urban districts, public hydrants were only turned on for an hour a day. Mobs of people wielding buckets battled for any water at all, never mind water for a bath. The rich did bathe, but only in cold water for medicinal reasons. The bath as we know it didn't emerge until mid-century when cities began laying down public waterworks to help combat filth and disease.

In the late nineteenth century, "bath" rooms were usually converted bedrooms close to the kitchen. Water was heated on the stove and then carried to the tub in buckets. But some bathtubs could heat water on the spot. Gas furnaces were placed directly under metal baths, turning them into giant saucepans. The risks were obvious. Eventually, the safer idea arose to pipe water through the house from a central boiler. Early boilers sometimes exploded, but improved designs made dependable hot water a reality by the 1870s. Having hot water on tap greatly increased the privacy of a bath since servants were no longer needed to carry water. In the early twentieth century, the mass production of pipes and fixtures made home plumbing affordable to all but the very poorest in society.

## boring ideas

In Colonial America, water pipes were not made of metal, but bored-out logs. Not surprisingly, they were often infested with insects and left water with a "woody" taste.

Although the nineteenth century ushered in a new era of public waterworks, plumbing was actually a long lost art. Clay pipes carrying running water first appeared in Pakistan around 2700 b.c. Metal pipes, made of folded copper sheets, debuted in Egypt around 2450 b.c. At its peak, Rome's elaborate system of aqueducts was supplying three hundred gallons of water daily for each citizen, nearly the amount an American family of four uses today. Ironically, Rome's hedonistic love of bathing may have contributed to its fall, which lead to centuries of squalor in the West until the rebirth of plumbing in modern times.

## cold comfort

In ancient Greece, hot water was available in some public baths, but most people preferred cold baths. The Greeks believed that cold water cured a variety of ills, and the Spartans even argued that using hot water was "effeminate."

## working on the chain gang

King Herod built the fortress of Masada in the first century B.C. on a steep hill atop the Dead Sea. It had a poor water supply, so Herod ordered a human chain comprised of hundreds, maybe thousands, of slaves to bring up water from below every day.

## a big drip

In many cities, underground pipelines were installed more than a century ago. Studies suggest that old, leaky pipes cost some major cities up to 30 percent of their daily fresh water supply.

## size matters

Ancient Roman landowners were able to get running water for their homes if they applied to the emperor for permission. Private pipes were linked with the main water line, and homeowners paid taxes according to the diameter of the pipe.

## plumbing the past

Lead was a popular material for pipes in the ancient world since it was pliable and rust-proof. In some European languages, the word "plumbing" comes from the Latin *plumbus*, meaning "lead."

# shampoo

Some poor souls spend huge amounts of time and money trying to revitalize and rejuvenate their hair, but it's impossible to breathe life back into it—hair is dead. The best we can do is rinse away the hair's natural sebum oil and the dirt, dead cells, and hair care products that stick to it. Early peoples such as the Phoenicians of the Middle East and the Scythians of southern Russia washed their hair with soap, but they had to put up with the tenacious scum that forms when soap is used in hard water. Before World War II when washing hair with soap was still common, some people collected soft rain water to minimize the scum. Others used vinegar, lemon juice, beer, and other mildly acidic solutions to rinse away soap deposits. Today, we have the luxury of a much more effective hair cleanser: shampoo.

Shampoos are detergents—a fact that shampoo-makers downplay for fear that consumers will confuse hair care products with harsher household cleaners. But detergents are simply cleansers that don't form sticky films in hard water. The first synthetic detergents were developed by the Germans during World War I. Since the regular supply of fats needed to make machine lubricants was cut off, soap fats were used instead. The resulting shortage of soap and the military's desire to find a cleanser effective in hard sea water sparked research into detergents. German chemists thought they were simply looking for an ersatz cleanser to get through the war, but the residue-free detergents they invented would go on to replace soap for many tasks by the 1950s, including washing hair.

Modern shampoos contain a host of natural ingredients such as herbs, balsam, and aloe vera intended to catch a shopper's eye. Many of these ingredients affect the smell and color of a shampoo, but not its cleaning power. Synthetics do the cleaning. Though fragrances and coloring make up less than 1 percent of a shampoo, they influence over 90 percent of all shampoo purchases.

## wash like an egyptian

The ancient Egyptians washed their hair with water and citrus juices. The acid in the citrus juices helped remove sebum oil from the hair.

90

## american beauty

The man who first brought modern shampoo to America was Dr. John H. Breck. From the 1930s to the 1970s, the company's ads featured portraits of "Breck Girls" painted by Charles Sheldon. More than three hundred portraits can be viewed at the Smithsonian.

## lather blather

Lather forms when detergent molecules surround air instead of oil. Although many people think that thick lather is a sign of a good shampoo, lather has little to do with a shampoo's ability to clean.

## malaysian persuasion

A Malaysian shopping mall holds the record for the most heads shampooed in one day: 1,068. Incidentally, this total is one less than the record number of weddings in which the same person has served as the best man—another dubious Malaysian feat.

## blood, sweat, and no more tears

Johnson's Baby Shampoo's "No More Tears" formula debuted in 1954, but product development began two decades earlier. The hard work paid off. The shampoo enjoyed a stint in the 1970s as the top-selling American shampoo.

## odds and healthy ends

The word "shampoo" comes from the Hindu word *champo*, which means "to massage." The first two-in-one shampoo (with conditioner), Pert Plus, was launched in 1987.

# showers

If showering is simply defined as washing with water dropped from over-head, then many early cultures can stake a claim to inventing the shower. A bathroom found in Egypt dating from 1350 B.C. had a shallow limestone basin where attendants poured jugs of water over a bather. Similar structures have been found in Mesopotamia and India. The first fully plumbed showers, however, were built by the ancient Greeks. Vase paintings from the fourth century B.C. show that water was piped into gymnasium showers through overhead mains. The water then cascaded down onto bathers through the mouths of gargoyles.

In the nineteenth century, most homes still had no proper bathroom, but the resurgence of bathing in the West sparked a proliferation of shower designs. The simplest ones consisted of a shallow tub with a water tank raised above it on metal legs. The water fell from the tank and was then forced back to the top with a hand pump. The English began building fancier showers that enclosed half of a bathtub by the late 1800s. These "hooded baths" clad in ornately carved mahogany resembled sombre confessional boxes, and were soon replaced by unadorned hoods of cast-iron.

Popular wisdom of the day held that the pressure of a shower spray was too much for the "weaker sex," who were warned to shower only under the advice of a physician. Equal-opportunity washing came in the 1910s when the modern shower emerged in the United States. Standardized fixtures and the use of tiles allowed showers to be built right into recessed walls, which lead to a showering boom for men and women alike.

So what cleans better, a shower or a bath? Definitely a bath. Soaking in a bath fully hydrates the skin, which makes it easier to scrub away dead skin cells. But soap and dirt float in bathwater and coat your body as you get up from the tub. So if you're really neurotic about getting clean, take a bath first and then rinse off in the shower.

## out of the woods

If they had been camping outdoors for a week, American men would be willing to part with an average of $7.90 for a hot shower. Women would be willing to fork over $8.70.

## civic snub

In 1812, the request by the Mayor of London to have a shower installed in his official residence was refused because "the want thereof has never been complained of."

## the water cycle

Some early showers reused drained water by pumping it back up to the water tank. A French model shown at the Paris Exhibition of 1900 required bathers to pump the water by pedaling a stationary bicycle.

## for the birds

Nineteenth century "cage" showers had an array of pipes twisted into something resembling a human-sized birdcage. These "therapeutic" cleaning machines not only had overhead sprays, but also separate kidney, spine, and bidet sprays, each with their own controls.

## just the facts, ma'am

Surveys have discovered that 57 percent of Americans shower daily, 17 percent sing in the shower, 4 percent shower with the lights off, and 3 percent clean their pets by showering with them.

## twist of fate

The first pressure-control showerhead that could be adjusted with a simple twist was developed by the German manufacturer Hansgrohe in 1968. More than seventeen million have been sold to date.

# sinks

Before the advent of indoor plumbing in the late 1800s, the vast majority of homes in the world had no room solely devoted to washing. With the notable exception of the Minoan Kings and Queens of the second millennium B.C., who had bathrooms, most people washed in various rooms with portable bowls and jugs of water. In medieval Europe, washbasins were popular because forks weren't; it was forbidden to touch God-given food with anything other than one's God-given hands. At the table, diners dipped their fingers into a common washbowl before and after meals. Washing hands with someone of the opposite sex became a popular ritual, and a refusal to do so was seen as a calculated slap in the face.

In the mid-1700s, British and French designers hoping to give the humble washbowl a dash of elegance began setting metal or china basins on dainty tripods made of carved wood. These three-legged stands had shelves for holding toilet knickknacks, and were placed in bedrooms and dressing rooms. Before waterproof tops were introduced, people wary of ruining their wood stands rarely indulged in a hearty splash of water.

Spindly washstands were replaced in the early 1800s with hulking pieces of furniture featuring marble tops and tiled backsplashes that allowed people to slosh water around with much more abandon. However, water still had to be poured in and out of most basins by hand. It wasn't until running water reached homes in England after 1870 that the true sink emerged. Sinks with plumbed taps soon found a permanent home in the newly created bathroom, and down-pipes fitted into basins drained waste water away easily. The English fancied opulent washstands of carved mahogany or embossed cast-iron, but the Americans favored mass-produced, functional sinks. Yankee minimalism (which spawned the all-white, tiled bathroom) won out by 1910, and has set the tone for the look of sinks and bathrooms ever since.

## design flaw

In the 1930s, Kohler and American Standard both launched "dental lavatories," small sinks just for brushing teeth. The public gave the idea a swift brush off.

## money down the drain

German manufacturer Nevobad offers a sink faucet made of 3.3 ounces of pure gold and a choice of 486 emeralds, sapphires, rubies, or diamonds. Most of us, however, would have to sell our homes to afford the $250,000 price tag.

## swinging both ways

In the early twentieth century, various space-saving designs involving hinged sinks were developed. To use the sink, it had to be positioned above the toilet (where water from the sink drained into). To use the toilet, the sink had to be swung aside.

## the right stuff

As everyone knows, the hot-water spigot is on the left while the cold-water spigot is on the right. This is because before the days of hot water there was only a cold-water spigot, and since most people were right-handed, it was put on the right.

## less is more

A prefab floor-to-ceiling washbasin and cabinet unit designed by American George Sakier in 1934 had a simple rectangular sink set on tubular chrome legs. It became a classic of sink design and was even displayed in New York's Museum of Modern Art.

## having a familiar ring

A four thousand-year-old stone sink with metal faucets was found in a tomb in the ancient Egyptian city of Thebes. The sink even had a plug for the drain that was chained to a bronze ring connected to the sink.

# soap

German chemist Justus von Liebig declared in the nineteenth century that the wealthiest and most enlightened nations would be the ones consuming the greatest quantities of soap. Since von Liebig set the standard for civility, more than thirty billion bars of Ivory Soap alone have been consumed around the world. Today our near-obsessive regimes of lathering and scrubbing are so taken for granted, it's hard to imagine that affordable, mass-produced soap has been available only in the last two centuries. Many Americans believed in the early 1800s that dirt was somehow healthy. Soap-making back then remained largely a household chore performed only once a year before the spring clean. In Europe, soap was commercially available, but heavily taxed as a luxury item until the 1850s. Only in the twentieth century has the use of soap become a widespread global phenomenon.

The origins of soap are shrouded in mystery. According to Roman legend, soap was discovered around 1000 B.C. on Sapo Hill, where animal sacrifices took place. Melted animal fat and wood ashes often mixed into the clay soil of the Tiber River, and women washing downstream found that the resulting soapy ooze made their clothes come cleaner. However, jugs full of soap-like material have been unearthed in Mesopotamia that pre-date the Roman discovery by almost two thousand years. The ancient Germans and Gauls are also touted as the originators of soap, but they may have used it as a wound medication or hairstyling aid rather than a body cleanser.

What is known for certain is that in the twelfth century the first great centers of soap production rose in Marseilles, Genoa, and Venice—cities close to rich supplies of soap-making ingredients. It wasn't until the nineteenth century that substantial advances in soap technology finally allowed for industrialized production, which would soon make soap one of the most indispensable components of the modern bathroom.

## salt in the wound

Soap is formed by the neutralization reaction of an acid (e.g., animal fat) and a base (e.g., wood ashes). Chemically, then, soap is a salt.

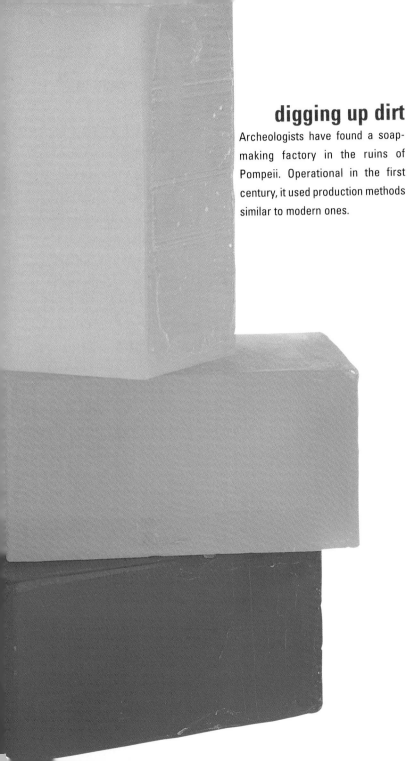

## not getting what you pay for

In a blind test conducted in 1990, *Consumer Reports* magazine found that the most expensive bar of soap, Eau de Gucci at 31 cents per hand-wash, rated dead last.

## digging up dirt

Archeologists have found a soap-making factory in the ruins of Pompeii. Operational in the first century, it used production methods similar to modern ones.

## hard act to follow

When Western standards of personal hygiene plummeted during the Dark Ages, the Arabs picked up the slack. They were the first to produce hard bars of soap, and by the tenth century, soap-making had become an important industry in the Muslim world.

## just curious

Ivory soap is "99$\frac{44}{100}$ percent pure." Have you ever wondered what's 56/100 percent impure? Wonder no more:

| | |
|---|---|
| uncombined alkali | 0.11 percent |
| carbonates | 0.28 percent |
| mineral water | 0.17 percent |

## before glasnost

The Kremlin created the "revolutionary" *Glavperfume* movement in 1930 to encourage female Comrades to be feminine. In addition to perfume and cosmetics, *Glavperfume* authorities also supplied soap, but only enough for each Russian to get two bars a year.

# sponges

We know that most families have skeletons in the closet. What we may not know is that many families also have skeletons in the bathroom. Natural sponges that we use for washing and bathing are the skeletal remains of sea animals whose living tissues have rotted away. Their intricately webbed, amorphous framework is composed of spongin, a material similar to that of animal horns. There are thousands of species of sponges, but only a handful are considered marketable. Those from the Mediterranean Sea are the softest and most prized, while sponges from the West Indies are rougher and less durable.

Sponges were used for bathing by the ancients, but other scrubbers also were popular. Greeks and Romans used a curved metal tool called a strigil to scrape their skin clean. Visitors to Islamic bathhouses were rubbed down with blocks of pumice. The Finns used coarse flaxen towels, while the Japanese washed with small sacs of rice bran. It's the sponge, however, that has survived to become a staple of the modern bathroom.

The popularity of sponges has increased since the 1940s with the development of synthetic sponges, which are more affordable than natural ones. Human-made sponges are open-celled polymer foams. During production, small air bubbles are introduced into the foam, which then expands and develops a porous, water-absorbing structure.

Historically, American women have used sponges, cloths, and other washing aids more than women from other countries, and this has impacted shower gel sales. Shower gels have always sold well in Europe and Asia, but until recently did not sell well in the United States. Unlike their Asian and European counterparts, who don't mind washing with gel and their bare hands, American women use a washing aid 76 percent of the time. When shower gels were bundled with sponges and poufs in the 1990s, U.S. sales increased by almost 40 percent.

## antidepressant

During the Depression, sponges continued to sell well in the United States since many unemployed people bought them in hopes of finding work scrubbing floors.

## oldie but goodie

Except for water, stones, and mud, the sponge has been around longer than anything else in the bathroom. Fossil evidence shows that natural sponges have existed for at least six hundred million years.

## baby talk

Studies show that sponge-bathed babies cry much more than tub-bathed babies. This may be because sponge-bathed babies that are not properly covered lose body heat faster.

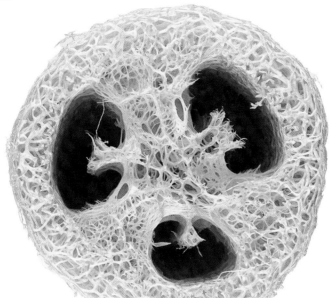

## back scrubber

Public toilets in ancient Rome did not have toilet paper. Instead, small sponges attached to sticks were provided for cleaning. The sponges were rinsed off in a channel of running water before use.

## false i.d.

It's easy to mistake a luffa (or loofah) for a sea sponge, since both have a webbed look and a squishy feel. A luffa, however, is really the insides of a cucumber-like gourd.

## open and shut cases

Synthetic sponges are open-cell foams, which are allowed to expand freely during production. Closed-cell foams are made by applying pressure, forming a denser material that is used for life-jackets and buoys.

# sunscreen

Lounging in the sun is largely a twentieth century phenomenon. Throughout history, people in various cultures went to great lengths to maintain that lofty emblem of the leisured class: a pasty complexion. Some smeared themselves with opaque creams which physically blocked sunlight, a tradition that dates back to at least 400 B.C. when the Greeks created a basic sunscreen of oil and sand. For the most part, however, heliophobic people simply wore long-sleeved clothing, hid under parasols, or cooped themselves up indoors.

Early in the twentieth century, only common field laborers had deep tans, but this began to change by the 1920s. Tanning grew more popular as railways began carrying large numbers of inland residents to beach resorts. Bathing suits also got progressively skimpier, revealing areas of skin that had never before seen the light of day. One of the first to capitalize on the new tanning craze was Monsieur Antoine de Paris, who created an orange tanning jelly for vacationers on the French Riviera which he named Bain de Soleil ("bath of the sun"). It encouraged rapid bronzing while protecting the skin from serious burns, and soon Europeans and Americans alike were clamoring for the "St. Tropez tan."

## skin irritation

The "Little Miss Coppertone" logo, created in 1953, featured a little girl with her shorts pulled down by a cocker spaniel. This exposed her white, untanned buttocks, prompting moralists of the day to charge the logo was "distasteful."

Modern sunscreens were first developed by the U.S. military during World War II. Since GIs stationed in the Pacific rarely found enough shade, the military tried to create a chemical sun-blocker instead. Red petrolatum, a petroleum by-product that blocked UV rays, was an early success. It was issued to pilots who were at risk of being shot down in the tropics. One of those who helped create red petrolatum was a Miami doctor, Benjamin Green. He also concocted sunscreens with cocoa butter, which he mixed in his wife's coffee pot and tested on his own bald head. In 1944, Green launched his homemade lotion as Coppertone. It was used by thousands of GIs during the war, and has been popular with millions of beach bums ever since.

### wild rice

Ron Rice, creator of Hawaiian Tropic sunscreen, cultivated an upscale mystique for his brand in the 1970s. Company literature boasted about Rice's fast cars and wild parties, and his beachfront home with fifty-six TVs.

### moonlighting

Wrinkling, sagging, and other signs of sun damage can be easily seen by comparing the skin on your face and buttocks. Though physiologically identical with facial skin, the skin on your bottom appears smoother because it is exposed to less light.

### beach bummer

Make sure children wear sunscreen. People with a history of sunburns in their youth have double the risk of melanoma later in life.

### something to reflect on

Skiers have plenty of reasons to slap on sunscreen. Fresh snow can reflect over 85 percent of sunlight, and UV radiation increases with altitude. At five thousand feet, UV rays are 20 percent stronger than at sea level.

### apocalypse later

Scientists predict that the sun will die in one thousand million years when it uses up its hydrogen. Just before the sun dies, nuclear reactions will create so much heat that the oceans will boil.

# thermometers

These days, a quick glance at a newspaper will tell you how cold it is in Alaska and how hot it is in Zaire. But at the start of the seventeenth century, people had no way of finding out the temperature of their own room, let alone that of exotic locales. Diagnosing body temperature was also a phantom science. In the absence of instruments that could quantify heat, doctors simply placed a hand on a patient's forehead and made their best guess.

A critical step towards measuring temperature was taken by Galileo in 1592. He invented a thermometer that measured heat based on the expansion and contraction of air. The device, however, had two drawbacks. First, it was not a sealed system, meaning the thermometer reacted to air pressure as well as temperature. Second, the inconsistent sizes of the thermometer tubes made it impossible to establish a reliable degree scale. Although Italian doctor Santorio Santorre created the first scaled air thermometer in 1612, accurately comparing the air temperature in two different cities remained a meteorologist's fantasy.

The air pressure problem was solved when Ferdinand II, Grand Duke of Tuscany, invented a sealed liquid thermometer in 1654. The problem of a reliable scale, however, was not solved until 1717 when Daniel Fahrenheit, a Dutch instrument maker, produced a set of identically sized mercury thermometers and devised a temperature scale that still bears his name. Anders Celsius, another eventual household name, developed the 100-degree scale in 1741 based on the freezing and boiling points of water. With the basic tenets of the thermometer established, scientists tinkered with improvements. One of them came when the aptly-named Sir Thomas C. Allbutt created the clinical thermometer in 1866. It gave an accurate reading in five minutes instead of the twenty needed by older devices, and it's the descendents of this thermometer that we place in our mouths (and other warm spots) today.

## bringing charges forward

The first electric thermometer was devised in 1822 by German T.J. Seebeck. It was able to gauge small temperature differences more accurately than mercury thermometers.

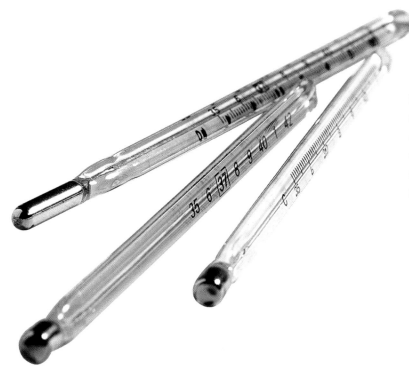

## spirited affair

Before mercury was used, thermometers contained a wide range of liquids. Seventeenth century craftsmen in Florence even made reliable thermometers containing red wine.

## a balanced diet

Santorio Santorre, creator of the scaled thermometer, once weighed his food intake and excretion by standing on a platform hung from the arm of a giant balance. His discovery that much of the food he ingested left the body by way of perspiration made him famous.

## hot tunes

A company in Dallas makes a baby thermometer which is hidden inside the nipple of a regular pacifier. If a baby's temperature is running high, the device plays a lullaby.

## in a world of one's own

Buzzard's Bay, Massachusetts, is home to The World's Only Thermometer Museum. With more than twenty-five hundred thermometers, its collection is touted as the biggest on the planet.

## reversal of fortune

Anders Celsius, the Swedish inventor of the centigrade scale, originally assigned 100 degrees to the freezing point and 0 degrees to the boiling point. After a few years, these values were finally switched.

# tiles

Glazed and colored tiles grew out of a long tradition of building with baked or sun-dried bricks in the Near East. The first colored glaze, a turquoise blue made of copper, was produced in Egypt as early as the fourth millennium b.c. Egyptian tiles depicted mythical beasts, real animals, and even slaves of various races. In Babylon, the famed Tower of Babel also was built with glazed earthenware. By Greek and Roman times, however, the use of glazed tiles died out. But the Greeks and Romans did pioneer another rich tile tradition: sumptuous wall and floor mosaics made with marble and other colored stones.

Ceramic tile-making was revived by 1000 a.d. in the Islamic world, where tile art reached a degree of technical and aesthetic sophistication that would surely have pleased Allah. In religious buildings, the finest tiles were used to create the *mihrab*, a lavishly decorated niche showing the direction of Mecca. The sumptuous colors used in Islam contrasted sharply with the drab earth tones of paving tiles in medieval Europe. But as Islamic tastes spread to Europe through Italy and Moorish Spain, European tiles began to burgeon with color. By the Renaissance, majolica—tiles glazed with tin to create a white surface that could be hand-painted—began coming into vogue throughout Europe.

One of the great centers of majolica tile-making was the Netherlands. High quality "delftware" tiles (named after the town of Delft) were being made from the seventeenth century. The characteristic blue-on-white decorations that made delftware famous were inspired by Chinese porcelain. As the Dutch middle class prospered in the 1600s, luxuries such as tiles became more affordable. Majolica tiles were easily damaged underfoot, so Dutch homeowners began lining them on kitchen and cellar walls, one of the first widespread uses of tile as a moisture barrier. When bathrooms emerged in the late 1800s, waterproofing surfaces with ceramic, stone, and glass tiles became the obvious choice.

## employment benefits

In the ancient world, the lives of skilled artisans such as tile-makers were often spared when invaders plundered cities. The artisans were carried off as part of the booty and made to serve their conquerors instead.

### the artful dodger

The quarries of Carrara, Italy, have produced more marble than any other site on earth. Local lore has it that Michelangelo himself narrowly escaped death twice at the quarries by dodging runaway blocks of stone.

### primary real estate

In important quarters of ancient Babylon, various structures were coded with color-glazed bricks. City walls were yellow, gateways blue, and palaces red.

### vaults of money

By the fourth century A.D., Roman artisans doing wall or vault mosaics were being paid 20 percent more than those doing floor mosaics. This was either because working "high up" was dangerous, or because floors, which were walked on, had lower status.

### dramatis personale

In the 1700s, English tiles were often decorated with landscapes. More offbeat tiles, however, portrayed various English actors in stage roles. The names of the actor and the play were often included as well.

### game over

Dutch tiles of the 1700s often depicted tulips, ships, and children's games. Some games, such as golf, are still recognizable. Others, like flying live birds with a string tied to one leg, are not.

# toilet paper

Toilet paper flies off the shelves of today's supermarkets faster than any other non-food item. But when toilet paper was first introduced to consumers in the mid-nineteenth century, sales were disastrous. Victorian-era Britons were too prudish to buy it, while Americans were too pragmatic; they couldn't fathom spending money on clean paper when old catalogs and newspapers could do the job. In fact, when mail-order companies switched from newsprint to glossy paper for their catalogs, many Americans complained that the pages could no longer serve double-duty.

The idea of buying toilet paper began to catch on in the late 1800s as more and more homes did away with chamber pots and outhouses and embraced the wonders of indoor plumbing. Modern bathrooms demanded modern accoutrements. The Scott brothers of New York became the first toilet paper success story when they launched their tissues in 1879. By the early twentieth century, toilet paper had become so lucrative that the Scott brothers began disparaging upstart brands with the ad slogan: "They have a pretty house, Mother, but their bathroom paper hurts." The market for such an essential product, however, proved big enough to support many competitors.

Though toilet paper was not mass-marketed until the 1800s, it was invented as early as 500 a.d. Unfortunately, it was only for the exclusive use of the imperial court of China—720,000 sheets of toilet paper were being produced annually for the court by the 1300s, while special perfumed tissues were being made for the imperial family. The rest of our ancestors were left to toil with leaves, stones, sticks, moss, and hay. Mussel shells were popular in coastal areas, while coconut husks found favor in the tropics. Medieval monks preferred pottery shards, and colonial Americans even used corn cobs. Alas, we can only imagine the pain and humiliation the world could have been saved if the imperial Chinese had only shared.

## the holey father

The idea of a perforated toilet roll that could be torn into small sheets was conceived by British manufacturer Walter Alcock. He unveiled his brainchild in 1879.

## different strokes

Surveys suggest that roughly half of all Americans neatly fold their toilet paper before use, about a third crumple it into a ball, and a small percentage wrap it around their fingers.

## stay on the right track

In parts of India and the Arab world, the right hand is traditionally used for eating and the left hand is used for wiping after going to the toilet. Because of this distinction, passing food to someone with the left hand is considered an insult.

## pot-ty

In seventeenth century France, the ladies of the court of Louis XIV preferred wool and even lace for wiping purposes. The middle classes did not enjoy such luxury, and used unspun hemp instead.

## doing his duty

The earliest known record of toilet paper use was penned in 589 A.D. A Chinese court official mused, "Paper on which there are quotations or commentaries from the Five Classics or the names of sages, I dare not use for toilet purposes."

## touché

In a 1906 letter to one of this critics, German composer Max Reger offered this famous retort: "I am sitting in the smallest room of my house. I have your review before me. In a moment, it will be behind me."

# toilets

## taking the plunger

Plungers are normally used to unclog toilets, but they were also widely used in the early 1900s as mutes for brass instruments such as the trombone. The technique was popularized by big bands such as Duke Ellington's.

The indignity of having to run outside every time nature called was first spared when crude indoor latrines were built on the Orkney Islands off Scotland around 2800 B.C. Drains were connected to recesses in stone walls, and users likely squatted over these primitive toilets. The first seated toilets were devised three hundred years later in what is now Pakistan. Elegantly made stone toilets with wooden seats were built in homes in the ancient city of Mohenjo-Daro. Sewage fell down through vertical chutes connected to street drains or underground pits. The very first flush toilet, which had an overhead water reservoir, was installed in the palace of Knossos on Crete around 1800 B.C. The ancient Romans favored communal toilets—ten to twenty to a room—where people unabashedly chatted and socialized.

When Europeans rebuffed all sensible ideas during the Middle Ages, the flush toilet vanished. People made do with chamber pots, which were wantonly emptied into stinking cesspits otherwise known as streets. The custom of a man walking on the side of a woman nearest the street arose since this position made the chivalrous man much more vulnerable to falling refuse. Even the opulent palace of Versailles, built in 1661, had no toilets at first, and residents and guests alike were expected to fertilize the outdoor shrubbery instead.

The flush toilet was re-invented in 1596 by Sir John Harrington, Queen Elizabeth's godson, but it failed to catch on. Elizabeth had one put in her palace, but she lamented that the rank odors wafting up from the cesspool discouraged her from using the toilet. The smell problem was solved in 1775 when British watchmaker Alexander Cummings invented a toilet drain with a U-bend that held a small amount of water which sealed off odors from below. Although the basic concept was re-born, the flush toilet would not become standard in homes until well into the twentieth century. In the twenty-first century, we can hardly imagine life without it.

### pipe down

Centuries ago, wealthy Chinese men urinated through foot-long, hollow lacquer tubes to keep their sprinkle on target. In the Near East, wooden pipes held in place with bandages were used instead of diapers to guide urine out of a baby's cradle at night.

### we're not in kansas

Japan's toilets are the most high-tech in the world. Some toilets have buttons that produce flushing sounds to mask unflattering bathroom noises. Toto, Japan's largest toilet company, is even developing home toilets that will chemically analyze urine.

### eternal bliss

The Egyptians used crude toilets that were rarely hooked up to sewer lines and were cleaned out by hand instead. The earliest surviving examples were found in tombs, buried with the dead for use in the afterlife.

### target practice

Eighteenth and nineteenth century European chamber pots were sometimes decorated on the inside with portraits of despised enemies. In England, chamber pots featuring Napoleon's mug were particularly popular.

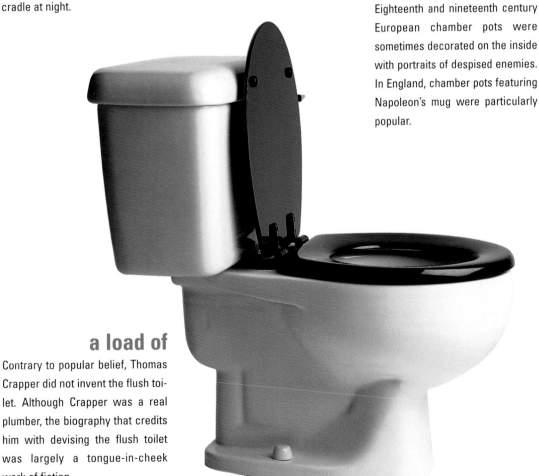

### a load of

Contrary to popular belief, Thomas Crapper did not invent the flush toilet. Although Crapper was a real plumber, the biography that credits him with devising the flush toilet was largely a tongue-in-cheek work of fiction.

# toothbrushes

Before the toothbrush there was the chew stick, a small twig with an end mashed into a frayed tuft that was used to scrub away prehistoric morning breath. The idea eventually trickled down to the Babylonians, Romans, and other ancients. The prophet Mohammed, an early champion of oral hygiene, used a chew stick called a *misswak* five times a day. He popularized it in the seventh century by telling the Islamic faithful that a prayer preceded by brushing was worth seventy ordinary prayers. Over a thousand years later, American Emily Thornwell was still trumpeting the virtues of the chew stick. In *The Lady's Guide to Perfect Gentility* (1856) she suggests, "A butcher's skewer must be bruised and bitten at the end, till with a little use it will become the softest and best brush."

The bristle brush that we know today was invented in China in the late 1400s, the finest of which featured hairs plucked from Chungking hogs. These new brushes spread to Europe by the 1600s, but remained high-priced novelties. Europeans who cared to clean their teeth in those days mostly toiled with rags. By 1755, Samuel Johnson's dictionary still made no mention of toothbrushes. But everything changed when Englishman William Addis re-invented the bristle brush in 1770 while serving time in Newgate Prison for starting a riot. When he was set free, he turned penance into profit by establishing the first company to manufacture toothbrushes in large quantities.

The modern toothbrush appeared in 1938 when Du Pont unveiled a nylon bristle brush: Dr. West's Miracle Tuft Toothbrush. Since then, the toothbrush industry has exploded, with more than three thousand toothbrush patents issued worldwide and yearly sales of $650 million in the United States alone. Profits would no doubt soar if Americans were more conscientious about changing their toothbrushes—the average is only twice a year.

## mr. manners

In *The Art of Love-Making*, Ovid, the Roman poet, offers this nugget of wisdom: "The girl who wishes to charm her lover should not brush her teeth in his presence."

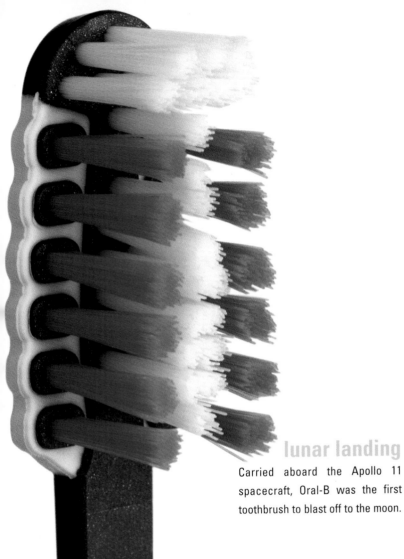

## power tool

Broxodent, the world's first successful electric toothbrush, was developed in Switzerland. Squibb and Company launched it to a happy American public in 1961.

## blowing smoke

In 1912, Congressman Cyrus Sulloway of New Hampshire declared, "I'd make it a penal offense for any mother to put a toothbrush in the mouth of a child." He lauded the cleaning power of chewing tobacco, setting an early precedent for the credibility of statements made by the tobacco lobby.

## lunar landing

Carried aboard the Apollo 11 spacecraft, Oral-B was the first toothbrush to blast off to the moon.

## instant karma

The fusayoji, or tufted toothpick, was brought to Japan in the seventeenth century by Buddhist priests from India. To dodge bad karma, superstitious users bent these early toothbrushes in half before throwing them away.

## making the grade

African-American educator Booker T. Washington was a zealous proponent of toothbrushing. Knowing this, some students arrived at Washington's school with a toothbrush and little else.

# toothpaste

Fossilized human teeth found in England reveal that tooth decay has hounded our kind for at least half a million years. Sadly, toothpaste has been with us for only four thousand of those years, while toothpaste that actually works has been around for even less time. Early toothpastes of dubious merit include an Egyptian recipe dating from 1500 B.C. featuring ground pebbles, crushed fruit, green rust, and honey. Hippocrates, the father of modern medicine, prescribed white stone, ground mice, and rabbit heads. Though these pastes may have helped clean through abrasion, they likely wore away precious tooth enamel as well.

The Romans also concocted their fair share of crackpot recipes, but some of their toothpastes did contain a genuine cleaning agent: human urine. Upper-class Romans coveted Portuguese urine in particular, which was touted as the strongest in Europe. This was likely true, but not because the Portuguese had prodigiously talented bladders. Evaporation during the long trip over land simply concentrated the liquid by the time it got to Rome. Urine, which contains the active cleanser ammonia, was used in toothpastes until the eighteenth century. Happily, the ammonia in today's toothpastes is synthetically produced.

The most important ingredient in modern toothpastes is fluoride. It helps minerals re-enter tooth enamel to repair cavities. Italian dentists first observed in 1802 that fluoride was present in tiny amounts in water, and that people living near fluoride-rich waters were cavity-free. These healthy teeth, though, were not pearly white but yellowy-brown since high levels of fluoride left tooth enamel mottled and stained. Despite the unsightly side effect, fluoride use for dental health was soon widely championed. Fluoride toothpaste can reduce tooth decay by as much as 30 percent. However, since most people brush for only a paltry minute, toothpaste is less important for clean teeth than a little more elbow grease.

## bad-mouthing

In the 1960s, volunteers who agreed to give up all oral hygiene for a clinical trial showed signs of gum disease within ten to twenty-one days. There was no word on when the bad breath began.

## armed to the teeth

After the end of the Second World War, the American military was left with thirty-four billion dollars worth of surplus supplies, including seven million tubes of unsqueezed toothpaste.

## say cheese

Isabella of Aragon (1470–1524), the wife of the Duke of Milan, used cuttlefish bone or pumice to polish her teeth and likely destroyed her enamel in the process. If Isabella was indeed the inspiration for the Mona Lisa as some suggest, a mouthful of hideous teeth would certainly explain her mysterious smile.

## devil-made-caries attitude

Up to World War II, Japanese nobles practiced an age-old custom of dyeing their teeth black. This was done for cosmetic reasons as well as to ward off the devil, who was thought to cause dental caries. Tests show that chemicals in the dye prevented cavities.

## down the tubes

In 1892, Dr. Sheffield's Creme Dentifrice (made in Connecticut) was the first toothpaste to be packaged in a collapsible metal tube. Dr. Sheffield's son got the idea from the metal tubes used for oil paints.

## dental records

Early abrasive toothpastes often left microscopic scratches on teeth. One famous set of ancient teeth, those of King Christian III of Denmark (1503–1559), show such telltale abrasions.

# towels

Pinning down the exact moment the towel was born is impossible. Textiles debuted ten thousand years ago, but no one knows when fabric was first used exclusively to dry the body. We do know, however, that the earliest woven fibers were flax, cotton, and silk, and they were no doubt used for towels. Egypt, known as the "land of linen," had flax fabrics by 4000 b.c. Spun cotton appeared in India around 3500 b.c., while silk debuted in China eight hundred years later.

In ancient Rome, bathing was ubiquitous and so were towels. The rich would bring two slaves to a public bath—one to guard clothes in the cloakroom and the other to carry towels. Petronius observed in the *Satyricon*, a satire of Roman life, that the most pompous bathers would only be dried with sheets of soft wool. After Rome's fall, baths vanished in Europe, but towels did not. In France, linen underwear often did double duty as a towel for rubbing off sweat; pageboys in wealthy English homes knelt in front of guests before dinner offering a bowl of water and a towel; and medieval engravings by German Albrecht Dürer show towels draped over wall-mounted racks no different from those today.

The art of drying off reached a zenith in Japan. Ancient shoguns did not use towels, but dressed in a succession of linen robes until dry. The *furoshiki* is a cloth used for wrapping and carrying toiletries, but it is also spread on the floor to dry the feet. The *tenugui* is small towel used to dry the body through repeated wiping and wringing. Since it does not get the skin totally dry, larger towels—praised as more "modern"—have now become popular.

Towels today are most often made of terry cloth, a cotton fabric first created in France in 1841. Some Europeans prefer flat-weave towels that look like tablecloths, but the trend in North America is towards fluffier, and thus heavier, towels. The world's largest towel plants now churn out more than one million pounds of finished towels every week.

## the color of money

Towels come in hundreds of colors, but deeper shades like navy blue, burgundy, and hunter green sell best. According to industry insiders, the top eight to ten colors generate 75 to 80 percent of total revenues.

## mystery miasma

Oddly, towels start to smell after just a few days, even though they only touch skin at its cleanest. This is because dead skin cells cling to moist towels, creating an ideal environment for the growth of mildew.

## goat coat

Olympic divers use highly absorbent shammies to dry off quickly. Shammies now can be made synthetically, but were originally made from the skin of the chamois, a goat-like animal from Europe.

## go with the flow

According to the rules of feng shui, the Chinese art of geomancy, pastel-colored towels balance cosmic energies in the bathroom. Blue towels are best. Because it is the color of water, blue will keep plumbing from clogging—and also improve cash flow.

## liberated

In 1994, President Bill Clinton and his entourage crossed the English Channel for D-Day commemorations in Normandy aboard the aircraft carrier George Washington. A few weeks later, White House staffers received a memo from the U.S. Navy demanding $562 for the embroidered towels and bathrobes missing from their staterooms.

## rough act to follow

In a traditional Finnish sauna, people beat themselves with birch twigs to promote blood circulation and sweating, then dry off with a rough towel made of flax and hemp.

# vaseline

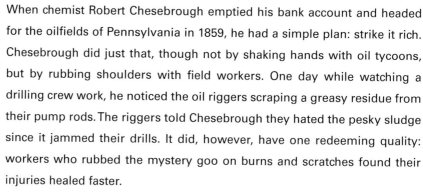

When chemist Robert Chesebrough emptied his bank account and headed for the oilfields of Pennsylvania in 1859, he had a simple plan: strike it rich. Chesebrough did just that, though not by shaking hands with oil tycoons, but by rubbing shoulders with field workers. One day while watching a drilling crew work, he noticed the oil riggers scraping a greasy residue from their pump rods. The riggers told Chesebrough they hated the pesky sludge since it jammed their drills. It did, however, have one redeeming quality: workers who rubbed the mystery goo on burns and scratches found their injuries healed faster.

Chesebrough quickly returned to his Brooklyn laboratory with a bucketful of the strange balm in hopes of isolating its key medicinal ingredient. After years of experimentation, he was able to extract a smooth, clear gel which he named "petroleum jelly." Unlike goose grease, garlic oil, and other rank nostrums of the nineteenth century, the jelly was pleasantly odorless. It also didn't spoil. To test his remedy, Chesebrough went far beyond the call of scientific duty and mutilated himself for weeks with blades, acids, and flames, inflicting all manner of cuts and burns to which he would apply his ointment. Each time, his wounds would heal rapidly and without infection. He also lingered around construction sites, treating workers' on-the-job injuries with equally amazing results.

## lateral thinking

Some of the more inventive documented uses of Vaseline include dabbing it on the faces of early silver screen stars to simulate tears, and smearing it on fishers' hooks to lure trout.

Chesebrough was convinced of the jelly's powers and set up a factory in 1870 to produce his new miracle salve: Vaseline. When initial sales floundered, he traveled up and down New York State in a horse-drawn wagon handing out free samples of Vaseline. His promotion worked. In less than a year, Chesebrough had a dozen horse-and-buggy salesmen selling Vaseline at the rate of one jar every minute. By the turn of the century, Vaseline was a household name and Chesebrough, as he had dreamed, was a wealthy man.

## some like it hot

Indigenous populations in the Amazon were so impressed with Vaseline's ability to resist spoiling—even under searing tropical heat—that they adopted Vaseline as a form of money.

## playing it cool

Arctic explorers have taken Vaseline with them on expeditions to the North Pole since it withstands freezing even at 40 degrees below zero.

## yummy in the tummy

Vaseline has countless uses, but researchers were shocked to discover that some people in the Amazon and India cooked with it. Robert Chesebrough was delighted, however, since he ate a spoonful of his invention every day for good health. He lived until the age of ninety-six.

## theory #1

The name Vaseline springs from the fact that its inventor, Robert Chesebrough, used his wife's vases to store the petroleum jelly in his lab. To "vase" he tacked on "ine," a commonly used medical suffix of the day.

## theory #2

The neologism Vaseline is a compound of words from two languages: *wasser*, the German word for "water," and *elaion*, the Greek word for "oil."

# wallpaper

Ever since we began surrounding ourselves with walls, we have had the irresistible urge to decorate them. The earliest adornments included woven grasses, animal skins, and cave paintings, which later evolved into more elaborate forms such as opulent stonework and wood paneling. Embroidered tapestries also were hung on walls, but were so expensive even the ritziest European monarchs had to drag entire sets around during their seasonal migrations from castle to castle. A cheaper alternative was hanging embossed leather. Cheaper still, however, was putting up paper that mimicked more lavish materials.

Because paper originated in China, many assume wallpaper is a Chinese invention. The Chinese did hang scrolls and banners on walls for funerals and festivals, but wallpaper as we know it today was a fifteenth century French invention. It was first made by the *dominotiers*, a guild of printers who also made domino papers (religious illustrations) and playing cards. Legally prohibited from printing lettering, the guild started out making end-papers for books and eventually larger "tapestry papers" for walls. Much of their work has not survived, and the earliest extant sample of wallpaper is instead of English origin. The design featuring a pomegranate motif was printed on used paper, which had traces of a poem lamenting the death of King Henry VII. This dates the wallpaper from around 1509.

Wallpapers were made by hand until the first wallpaper-printing machines debuted in 1785. Soon after, machines were devised to make endless rolls. This made wallpaper more affordable, but enraged artistic purists such as Englishman William Morris who railed against machine production. His wallpapers of the late 1800s were hand-printed, but this made—and still makes—his designs prohibitively expensive. A worker hand-printing a Morris reproduction today can complete thirty rolls of wallpaper a day. In the same time, a machine can churn out twenty miles.

## chinese smorgasbord

Paper was first created in China around 105 A.D. by Tsai Lun, an official of the Imperial Court. He made it from mulberry fibers, old rags, fish nets, and hemp waste.

## this is a holdup

A San Diego company makes a "fiber-reinforced polymer" wallpaper that can help hold buildings and bridges together during an earthquake. About as thick as a business card, it has already been applied to more than fifty bridges in California.

## same old, same old

In the late nineteenth century, the guru of the Arts and Crafts movement, Englishman William Morris, had his wallpaper designs carved into blocks of pearwood. The wood is so durable that many of the same blocks still are used for Morris reproductions today.

## overkill

Early wallpapers often were printed over banned literature. In 1673, the Bishop of London ordered copies of Thomas Hobbes's *Leviathan* to be printed over since the book argued the Church should be subordinate to the State.

## woe canada

In the 1940s, vignette papers were introduced that featured repeating scenes floating on colored backgrounds. In Canada, there were even papers with Mounties, dog sleds, and igloos.

## mood swings

Japanese scientists are working on technology that could give us "TV wallpaper" by 2010. Cardboard-thin screens fixed to walls or ceilings could instantly change the ambiance of a room by displaying different images.

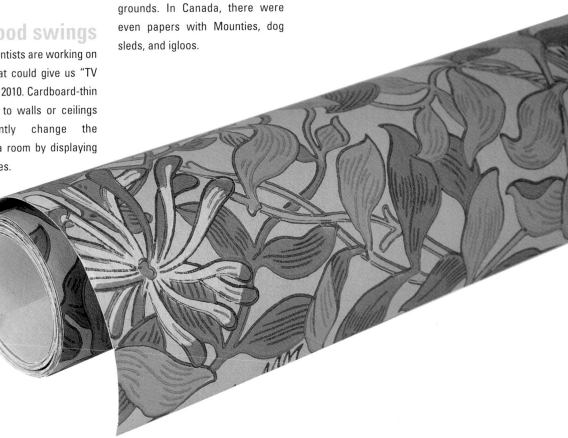

# wigs

The world has never quite been able to make up its mind about wigs. Considered swank in one era, then vulgar the next, wigs have been both loved and reviled through the ages. The story begins in Egypt, where wigs were being worn by 3000 B.C. Wigs made of human hair and plant fibers protected the scalp from the sun since it was common for both Egyptian men and women to shave their heads bald. In the first century B.C., dark-haired Roman women started a fad for blond wigs, which were made with tresses scalped from the heads of conquered Germans and Gauls. Roman men also wore wigs, but only to hide balding.

The use of wigs declined in Europe with the rise of the Christian Church, which condemned false hair as "hateful to Heaven." Christians who wore wigs, especially women, were accused of licentiousness, barred from church services, and even excommunicated.

Wigs finally made a comeback in the seventeenth century when a mania for "false heads" was spearheaded by two kings: Louis XIV of France and Charles II of England. Louis (going bald) and Charles (going gray) wore lush, voluminous wigs—a lead taken up by the wealthy and the working class alike. The trend spread across Europe and even to the American Colonies. Wigs became so commonplace by the eighteenth century that some homes even had wall pegs for visitors' hairpieces. In England, the demand for hair was so great that children walking alone on the street were in danger of having their hair surreptitiously snipped off. The wig craze came to an abrupt end in the 1790s when the French and American Revolutions turned all symbols of past regimes into fashion faux pas.

Except for a revival in the 1960s, the obvious head of false hair has not come back into vogue. Today, people who wear toupées or hair extensions do so discreetly. Whether people will ever again start flaunting overgrown wigs remains to be seen.

## hairbrush

Instead of wearing a wig, some bald Roman men simulated hair by painting their skulls.

### the glass menagerie

In the 1700s, women's wigs in Europe had become so outlandish that many were even decorated with blown glass figurines. Replicas perched atop women's heads included animals, cupids, nymphs, planets, hot-air balloons, and even tombstones.

### mark of distinction

In Japanese Kabuki theater, wigs are worn to clearly differentiate characters by age, sex, class, and occupation. Not to be short-changed, ghosts and other supernatural characters also wear identifying wigs.

### classic text

In his *Encyclopedia*, Diderot suggests that the worst quality hair for wigs comes from the heads of the sexually debauched, while the best quality hair comes from those who drink hearty amounts of beer and cider.

### deadly secret

Mary, Queen of Scots, was a devout wig-wearer. She wore an auburn wig so inconspicuously that even those close to her did not realize she donned false hair—until she was beheaded.

### beefing it up

In the early eighteenth century, European wigs sometimes stood two feet or taller atop the head. Since wigs were held in place with a gel made of beef marrow and were worn for weeks at a time, looking good came at the price of smelling bad.

# about the author

HOLMAN WANG is a teacher and a writer. He has a bachelor's degree in anthropology from the University of Toronto, and a bachelor's degree in education and a master's degree in architecture history from the University of British Columbia. When he is not writing, he enjoys traveling, riding around town on his Vespa scooter, and brushing his teeth. He lives in Vancouver, Canada.

# about the photographers

T.J. ADEL and SAMUEL DULMAGE have been working together at T.J. Adel & Son Photographics Limited in Vancouver, Canada, for over ten years. They specialize in shooting art, artifacts, products, and architecture. They have extensive experience shooting micro-diamonds and other small pieces of jewellery. They would like to thank the designers of the Mamiya KL 140mm F4.5 M/L-A Macro Lens, which was invaluable for producing many of the high quality close-ups in *Bathroom Stuff*.